TRANSCENDING Sexual Trauma

Dina Saalisi

Self-Awareness Tools and Nature-Based Practices to Cultivate Inner Healing

Including 16 Experiential Practices and 22 Flower Remedies for Emotional Support

REDFeather®
MIND | BODY | SPIRIT
4880 Lower Valley Road, Atglen, PA 19310

Library of Congress Control Number: 2025932299

Edited by Crystal Mannara
Designed by Alexa Harris
Type set in The Seasons / Corporate S
Original watercolor paintings on page 23 and page 72 by Obi Kaufmann
Photos on the following pages are courtesy of the author: 15, 101, 102, 103, 104, 108, 109, 110, 111, 112, 113, 115, 116, 118, 119, and 121.

ISBN: 978-0-7643-7037-3
ePub: 978-1-5073-0591-1
Printed in China

10 9 8 7 6 5 4 3 2 1

MIX
Paper | Supporting responsible forestry
FSC® C167893

Published by REDFeather Mind, Body, Spirit
An imprint of Schiffer Publishing, Ltd.
4880 Lower Valley Road
Atglen, PA 19310
Phone: (610) 593-1777; Fax: (610) 593-2002
Email: Info@redfeathermbs.com
Web: www.redfeathermbs.com

Table of Contents

For every woman who has ever been violated emotionally, physically, or psychically. For every woman.

Acknowledgments

I've had many teachers along my path, some whom I never met in person but whose philosophies and insights reached me through their writings. Others I connected with in face-to-face conversations, where their teachings deeply touched me. I'm forever inspired by and profoundly grateful to all those who've mentored me, offering their unique wisdom, which has shaped me and sparked my growth.

My work in the world is able to come to fruition through the beautiful constancy and devoted support of my family. With unconditional love for David, Max, Isra, Jim, Amanda, and Winnie, who have lifted me up throughout the years, joined in belly-bursting laughter, offered me deep tenderness, and accepted my loving care in return.

In loving memory of Mom and Gram.

May all beings have happiness and the causes of happiness.

May all beings be free from suffering and the causes of suffering.

May all beings rejoice in the well-being of others.

May all beings live in peace, free from greed and hatred.

–Siddhartha Gautama, the Buddha; excerpted from *The Four Immeasurables*

Preface

There is no linear path to healing from sexual trauma. It's an adventurous terrain that everyone encounters differently. Some of my greatest growth has come about in fits and starts, with new awareness arising at any given time, sometimes in between long periods of pause and reflection. One thing I've learned over the years is that healing happens when I take responsibility for my wounds. Never the victim's fault, "responsibility" means seeking ways to heal, and taking time to care for yourself, as an ongoing practice. As you do the work to transcend your suffering, allow yourself to dance to your own rhythm, meander in the magic of your soul-scape, explore your deeper wisdom, indulge in the beauty of messiness, and find the meaning in your fluid process of healing.

To overcome the battering effects of sexual trauma means to go beyond survival mode and develop an unshakable foundation of resilience. Through psychospiritual practices you get to know yourself better, gain inner strength, and befriend all of your parts. Instead of trying to fix what's broken, you begin to honor your wounds as opportunities for growth, and you begin to truly heal. This is a radical shift from merely surviving, to *thriving.* Working from a body-mind-nature connection, you attune your physical being to receive all the messages available within yourself, as well as within your natural surroundings, in order to foundationally engage healing.

In my efforts to serve as many people as possible with this nourishing wisdom, I was called to create a handbook that is concise, relatable, and powerful. The simplicity found in these pages is meant to navigate you through a rewarding process, filled with great luminosity and profound depth. Some days will feel harder than others. That never goes away, but the comfort is in knowing that healing is within your grasp, is part of your soul journey, and can be realized through a gentle approach that takes into account the arc of your whole experience, to include all of your challenges as fuel for transformation.

This book speaks directly to the sexual trauma specifically suffered by women. Indeed, I feel that anyone who has experienced sexual trauma, regardless of their gender, will benefit from this guide. But I also felt strongly about creating an exclusive sanctuary for women, as part of the deeper exploration of female empowerment. This book is written with women readers particularly in mind, since I wanted to be able to uniquely speak to women's experiences and create a "safe space" for their empowerment. Readers of all genders may benefit from these techniques, however, and my hope is that this book finds its way into the hands of all abuse survivors, who will flourish in its wisdom. That said, I do believe there is a collective "feminine" energy that people of all genders possess and can learn how to work with in order to heal. I encourage people of all genders to find their own path toward healing, within these pages.

When you embark on an adventure toward deeper healing, you may notice that vulnerabilities, old patterns, and trauma triggers arise throughout the process. Sometimes psychospiritual practices and subtle energy medicines will create short states of imbalance before bringing you into greater balance. This is referred to as a "healing crisis" and can be worked through with basic self-soothing techniques such as grounding into Nature, drinking plenty of water, eating a light and nourishing meal, and getting rest. Remember to ease up when needed, and always work at your own pace.

There are sixteen practices offered within these pages, designed by me as the result of a combination of modalities learned over decades of my own healing work with various guides, and informed by my ongoing witnessing of others. The parts of the text in italics are excerpts from my personal journals composed over the course of thirty-five years.

The exercises and suggestions given in each chapter are for when you've already set out on a path of recovery. This guide is not intended for when you are in the active throes of sexual trauma or experiencing symptoms of posttraumatic stress disorder (PTSD). Please make sure that you have compassionate, skilled, emotional support in place before engaging in the practices outlined in this book.

I am not a licensed medical doctor or psychotherapist. I am a sexual-trauma survivor. For over four decades, I've worked with various practitioners to hone my healing skills, as I developed my gifts for leading others to create wholeness of being. With certifications as a trauma-informed health-and-wellness coach, flower therapy practitioner, and hypnotherapist, I continue to grow and evolve alongside those on the path of transcendence.

A Note on Sexuality

All beings have a unique sexual energy that contains all of their attitudes, ideas, feelings, behaviors, and experiences connected to the physical, emotional, and social aspects of intimacy. As an abuse survivor, you may be disconnected from this part of your innate being. To reclaim your sexuality may be one of the most profound aspects of your healing journey, with ebbs and flows informed by your individual needs, which shift over time. This guide will help you transcend the aftereffects of sexual trauma, but it won't lead you through your distinctive personal process of accepting and honoring the complex facets of your sexuality. As you seek deeper awareness of what holds you back from connecting with your divine essence, you will be able to apply the methods of transcendence in this book to any emotional challenges that arise related to your sexuality.

Our Greater-Than-Human Family

One thing I know to be true is that the more I lean into and connect with the energies of Nature, the easier life is. Since witnessing the stories of sexual trauma from hundreds of women, whenever I ask, "When do you feel the most at ease?," the answer is almost exclusively, "When I'm in Nature." This is why the subtitle of the book calls out Nature as part of the healing equation of body and mind. On the days that my struggles are palpable, my flow derailed, I'm always willing and ever grateful to be able to go outside and feel held in the reciprocal communion of my nonhuman family. Quickly and effortlessly, I find restoration, as my eyes witness the plants and animals nearby and I give my attention over to my kindred beings. Some days these are the only relationships that feel right, since the connections often lead me to know what to do for myself to get back into a healthful rhythm.

To be able to cultivate my innate, nourishing attachment to all of Earth's beings is to create a community that will always support me to thrive and never abandon me. I know that I will always find solace and strength in knowing that there is a higher power that is tangible and easily accessible, right in my own backyard.

The Language of Nature

As I treasure the dynamic interplay of words, feelings, and thoughts, I'm acutely aware of the lack of language to express deeper sentiments of such liminal states, such as when connecting with the nonhuman elements of the world. Much of the work and awareness that surrounds transcending trauma is rooted in the profound wisdom of spiritual experience. Often, words fail.

One such word, "Nature," although part of the subtitle of this book, falls flat in elucidating the essence of our omnipotent, quantum, life-force energy. The contrite term "Nature Lover" means someone who really digs nature and hikes or takes pictures of landscapes as a hobby—as if it were a marginalized experience, to *love* Nature. Recently I had a revelation about this term of endearment and understood it to mean Nature Lover as in Nature (is my) Lover. I adore them, serve them, and continually feel passion for and consummation with them as I am held in the safety of their warm and wild embrace. In this way, I offer the word "Nature" as an understandable concept that can be expanded on by way of sentient awareness. Notice that whenever I refer to Nature throughout the book, I capitalize the word as a proper noun, as I do Moon, Sun, Bee, Rose, and so on. This is an animistic lens, set in focus and upheld by most world cultures, present and past. When I practice using language that treats the collective of all beings on Earth as alive, sacred, and synergistic, I offer you an opportunity to reflect on your place within our universal family and how the energies of Nature support this organic interrelationship.

The current scientific research on the benefits of being in Nature shines a broad light on the many ways it contributes to emotional, spiritual, and physical health. Countries such as Japan, Finland, and South Korea have national policies that make Nature-based practices and resources accessible to their citizens as an underpinning of physical and emotional well-being. According to numerous studies published by the US National Library of Medicine on the physical effects of "grounding" in Nature, the myriad benefits include improved sleep, normalized cortisol levels, reduced pain, reduced stress, improved digestion, and, perhaps most importantly, an enhanced ability for the autonomic nervous system to shift from sympathetic to parasympathetic activation. What this means for trauma survivors is that spending time in Nature triggers a physiological reaction toward stasis where your body and mind become more balanced, and your healing capacity increases. So, the more you go out into Nature and activate this positive response, the more you develop a tranquil inner state and the less likely you are to get stuck in trauma triggers.

In addition to Nature contributing to physical healing, connecting with the energies of Nature in a spiritual sense enhances body and mind health. Quantum physics understands that all living organisms are essentially connected in a constant exchange of energy, sharing one vital field of experience. A felt essence that flows between Nature and the human etheric body naturally provides a sense of balance, inner strength, and harmony. I call myself an "energeticist," and what this means to me is that I can easily connect with the energies of my surroundings and recognize the alliances found within the various elemental facets of Nature. Through the years, I've learned that when I set an intention to connect deeply with the essences of Nature, I catalyze the medicine of well-being within myself. The practices in this book help you attune to a sense of harmony within your energetic body, through an array of mental and physical experiences, grounded in the spiritual medicine of Nature.

Finally, the addendum is dedicated to the indications for the use of twenty-two flower remedies. Flower remedies are energetic plant medicines that are taken internally to support well-being at any stage of recovery. In my decades-long experience in working with these tinctures, both personally and professionally, I've witnessed time and again how they accelerate the healing process by providing nourishing support to the emotional body.

Introduction

As a small child who suffered sexual abuse, I learned at a young age how to "go inward" to escape the fear and terror I felt when among others. Raised Catholic, I was never much for church, but the one thing I picked up on was the power of prayer as a healing tool. Being a lover of words and books from an early age, I relished the idea of "rhyming couplets" casting an energetic boundary from the pains of the outer world. I spent countless hours in my room, alone, away from the heaviness of my family, where I found poetry a soothing ally.

"I love God and God loves me, and that's why I live happily." I made up this mantra and chanted it often as a self-soothing method when I was ten years old, after the sudden death of my father. What I realize now is that this chant not only provided a sense of safety by way of my inner strength but also connected me to a higher power that held me within a liminal space.

Many years later, as a new mother, suffering from sleep deprivation and no family allies to help carry the load, my trauma came bubbling up and engulfed me in a sea of despair most mornings. I clearly recall lying in bed, where I could hear the faint laughter of my husband and young son playing downstairs, and I just couldn't pry the covers off my pained body. I would stare out the window at the blue Sky and feel surges of resentment and anger that the day could be so beautiful when I felt so utterly miserable. As a poet, these words swirled through my mind: "*I hate you Sky for being so blue. Hey there, Mountain, fuck you too.*" The very existence of ethereal Sky and solid Mountain was an afront to the core of my being. Yet, somehow, it felt strangely empowering to utter this betrayal out loud. What I didn't realize at the time was that I was using the power of the spoken word to reinforce the idea that the world was cruel and that I deserved to suffer. But there was also a comfort in the rhythm of the words and the depth of suffering they conveyed, since often the bitter can be healing. It was like a reverse affirmation, which on some level jolted me awake with its severity, shifted my perspectives, and led me to reclaim the power that was usurped by what happened to me.

The stages of healing trauma are poignantly potent and somewhat mysterious, simultaneously pushing and pulling in competing directions. Once the fog of negativity was played out through my creative language, I realized that the vast blue Sky was there for me to relax into, that the Mountain stayed strong. They didn't abandon me as I hurled my disdain at them. In this light, I could see that their strength was there for me all along.

What Is Sexual Trauma?

When one's body and mind are impacted by sexual abuse, energetically the trauma lives in the ethereal body. This stored trauma causes the survivor to become trapped in insidious patterns that play on repeat, over and over, unconsciously deteriorating their sense of self-worth. To constantly have to soothe the little cuts of anger, resentment, depression, and anxiety is indeed a rollercoaster ride of oppression. To be able to walk down the street, be productive at work, and act joyfully in public, without the possibility of being catcalled, derided, or attacked, are basic human rights that women are robbed of daily.

I remember being pissed as a teenager at the idea that as a young woman, I was prey. Nearly every time I went out in public, sexual verbal abuse was hurled at me. I recall my looming depression and fear at such a horrifically acceptable, ongoing devaluation of my personhood. I'm not suggesting that the trauma associated with rape is the same as the traumatic derision suffered through catcalling, but I am saying that the pervasive quality of the accepted verbal sexual abuse of females quietly eats away at the humanity of womankind, every day. Learning how to silence the critical voices of self-doubt, low self-esteem, self-loathing, body dysmorphia, and fear can become a full-time job.

The personal is political. Transcending sexual trauma is partly about bringing awareness to the cultural conditioning of misogyny. The severe lack of information, and the widespread misinformation about women's bodies and experiences, contributes to the perpetual, systemic oppression we all suffer from. According to the National Sexual Violence Resource Center, in 2023 in the USA, 81% of women and 43% of men reported being the target of sexual violence. RAINN (Rape, Abuse, and Incest National Network) estimates that every sixty-eight seconds a woman is sexually assaulted. In recent years the awareness around sexual assault has risen, in large part behind the velocity of the #metoo movement in 2017. According to the 2024 "#MeToo Survey," conducted by Tulane University, 82% of women who were asked said they had suffered sexual assault at least once in their lives. Many victims do not report sexual assault but suffer in silence, so we can assume the rates are higher. Beyond sexual assault, violence toward women also extends into the ghastlier offense of "femicide." The intentional gender-related killing of women and girls topped the charts in 2022, with a whopping 89,000 lives lost internationally, mostly at the hands of husbands and boyfriends. I'm not including these gross details in a guide for healing to ignite terror or fear, but to shine a light on and bring candidly out into the open this significant, constant wounding of our culture that affects all beings on Earth.

With the prevalence of such a pandemic on the collective female body, the need for immediate solutions is obvious and crucial. Really, the ubiquity of sexual violence calls for awareness centers and healing outlets to become as commonplace as Starbucks. I'm not kidding, nor do I mean to compare sexual violence to coffee. I'm just saying that providing such a necessarily blatant amount of transparent information, care for victims, and support for survivors might begin to shift the negligent mindset around this ferocious brutality.

I can't help but feel personally attacked by the current sexual-assault statistics, and I wonder if perhaps we're looking at the wrong data in order to put an end to it. As usual, the statistics reflect the abundance of victims, but I'm pretty sure it's not just one perpetrator inflicting all of the violence. Where are the figures that reflect how many sex offenders are in our midst? Maybe if those chilling details were splashed on the front page of the papers, an incentive for change would be catalyzed.

Reclaiming What's Yours

Being in a female body continues to put me at risk of sexual violence, but with the grace of age and the courage of wisdom, I'm empowered to act from a place of inner strength. To me this means walking with my head high and knowing that on this rousing odyssey of deeper self-awareness, I've collected and honed the tools that will help me manage whatever challenges land in my path. Goddess forbid, no one wants to have to suffer violence, but I have, and I'm here now, living a whole, love-filled life. To know that I am capable of salvaging what at one time seemed too mangled to reconstruct is to experience true healing.

Transcending sexual trauma starts here. With the awareness that you are not alone, and that you need not endure pain in silence. A powerful resonance is alive in the knowing that most every other woman, to some degree, has experienced what you have. Although formed through a shared experience of suffering, the bond created with related survivors can move mountains. Your own boulders begin to feel less daunting as you are motivated to push uphill alongside others. There's a sense of solidarity that carries each of us further together than we could be lifted alone.

With love and flowers,

Dina Saalisi

St. Helena, California

December 2024

Chapter 1
Get to Know Yourself Better

I'm beginning to mourn the person I might never become. I squirm in the face of my discomfort. I want, no, I need, out. But really, in. Into a deeper sense of Self. I search for who I truly am under the façade of who I think I am. I traverse the depths of my soul beyond the shadowlands of what I think I know.

Self-awareness is the blade that cuts through deception. As a sexual abuse survivor, one of the most profound ways I found to reclaim my sense of wholeness was to get deeply, intimately close with myself. Not a lovey-dovey, superficial, self-indulgent sort of closeness, but the kind of devotion that holds my challenges and open wounds as the most-powerful parts of my being. To get to know, firsthand, the ugliness of the shame and guilt festering inside me, and to give it the respect it deserved, by dosing it with the medicine of self-acceptance, then watching it transform.

What I realized once I clearly saw the myriad, insidious ways in which my sexual trauma was spilling out all over the place was that I was living my whole life on the basis of what was done to me, which was not my true nature. As I began to question how and why my behaviors were keeping me hostage to a lesser way of being, I got more lucid about the ways the pain and trauma surfaced. It was as if the latent energy of my trauma, locked away for so long, came rushing forth with an urgency to be reckoned with, no matter what. A desperate blend of intuition mixed with naivete led me to somehow know that I needed to face my darkness within. As I got really good at dousing the looming shadows with burgeoning light, I began to alchemize the energies of fear and shame into the medicines of courage and confidence.

No Mud, No Lotus

One of the most beloved spiritual masters who has ever lived was Vietnamese Buddhist monk, peace activist, and teacher Thich Nhat Hahn. "No mud, no lotus" was a powerful teaching he liked to use as a metaphor for spiritual growth. The Lotus flower, symbolic of spiritual awakening and enlightenment, grows only in areas of shallow water no more than 5 feet deep, with 6 inches of mud at the bottom. The enormous seedpods are submerged completely beneath the water's surface during the dark of night, only to emerge clean and in glorious full bloom in the morning. Without the murky depths of the mud, the Lotus would not flourish. When you gaze at this surreal-looking blossom, with its golden seedpod center and glowing petals, you are witnessing a manifestation of the mud. The understanding is that you must traverse the muck of life and hold the deep parts of yourself that were violated in the tender arms of loving acceptance, to arrive at the majesty of the Lotus flower within.

Embody Healing with Subtle Energy Practices

> People don't need to be forced to grow. All we need is favorable circumstances: respect, love, honesty, and the space to explore.
>
> —Ellen Bass

All of your habits, thoughts, and beliefs occur at the unconscious layer of being. Without having to do anything, your actions, relationships, and life are commanded by an invisible force that catalogs every experience you've ever had. Neuroplasticity is the brain's ability to change its physical structure as a result of learning. The human brain was once considered pliable only at certain developmental stages, but science now recognizes it as malleable and able to change throughout a person's life, with the development of new perspectives and enhanced awareness. Being able to engage in an inner dialogue that reshapes your mind's ability to see things in a positive light, rather than getting stuck in thoughts that deteriorate your sense of who you truly are, is a powerful shift in perception.

The following chapters include guided visualization exercises meant to be enjoyed regularly. You can record each practice on your phone as you read it out loud, pausing briefly between sentences. Or you can have someone read the practice to you. This way, you can relax into the journey with your eyes closed. Make a commitment to yourself to spend at least fifteen minutes each day to consistently engage your healing practices. Create a private space in your home that will be your sanctuary, where you can hear your quiet, intuitive voice. Decorate the area with soft colors, textures, flowers, and images that feed your soul, and allow your deepest desires to manifest into being, and your inner knowing to emerge as absolute truth.

Some of the practices ask you to envision yourself and your challenges by using different lenses of awareness. The perceptions include "self," "other," and "observer." "Self" is who you are in your body, feeling your inner sensations, looking out through your eyes. "Other" can be another person or a feeling part of yourself, such as anger, fear, or sorrow. "Observer" is the witness, who views your "self" and the "other" and watches the scene unfold. As you engage in each exercise, do so with a sense of curiosity. There is no right or wrong way, and for each person what is needed is different. Embrace the practices as you see fit, trust that you always have the answers within, and recognize that you possess exactly what you need to grow, heal, and thrive.

Does engaging in psychospiritual practices mean that you will never meet adversity again? Of course not. But what it does mean is that when trauma triggers arise, you'll be well resourced to deal with them. So, then, transcending trauma isn't so much about living a perfectly harmonious life as much as it is about finding the joy within the disharmony of life. This is the essence of healing. Not to strive to fix or even to cure, but to embrace a mindset of growth and resilience, in the face of inevitable challenges.

Although it's important to create consistency with your practices, it's equally valuable to take one day a week "off" from your practice schedule and from your daily routines, to do only what feels most nourishing. This is a beautifully supportive practice in itself. I set aside Sundays as my day where I get to dawdle, tantalize my senses, and explore inspirations in each moment. This might mean delegating responsibilities to others, keeping my calendar open for spontaneous outings, wandering in Nature without an agenda, locking myself away in my personal sanctuary to create art, or perhaps do nothing. This negative space in my weekly routine ensures me time for rest, renewal, and replenishment, which carries me forward throughout the rest of my week. That said, I realize that my time became my own again once my kids grew into adulthood. It's likely that if you have young children or other demanding responsibilities, reserving an entire day will feel improbable, if not impossible. Have a light touch and get creative about taking small bites of time to honor the art of self-nourishment. Start with five-to-ten-minute mini moments scattered throughout your week, as you reflectively pause and ask yourself, "What would nourish me in this moment?" Feel into the energy of this desire and, if possible, honor your inner request. By giving yourself brief yet regular breaks to explore your deeper wishes in the present moment, you develop new neural pathways that create a sense of spaciousness within and can support you to carve out more space in your scheduled life.

The Foundation of Self-Nourishment

> Caring for myself is not self-indulgence, it is self-preservation, and that is an act of political warfare.
>
> —Audre Lorde

I love the idea that nourishment isn't only about consuming healthful foods, breathing clean air, and drinking pure water—on a much deeper level, it's about feeding your soul. It's about procuring habits, practices, and relationships that support you to live a healthy and meaningful life. How do you show up for yourself on a regular basis?

It's no surprise that survivors tend to continue cycles of neglect by ignoring our essential needs for pleasure and renewal. Putting others first for most of my life, I had a serious issue with being a "giver." It took me awhile to learn how to take in what I needed to thrive, since it was more comfortable to turn my attention outward than it was to accept my deeper desires.

To nourish myself from the nutritive depths of self-care was something that I learned to cultivate through a radical commitment to myself. A life-changing awareness came in the understanding that one of the best things I can give myself is time to reflect inwardly on my thoughts, feelings, and experiences with a compassionate gaze. In the beginning of my healing journey, I shifted the habit of self-neglect by dedicating a minimum of one hour every morning to engage in well-being practices. For years, I got out of bed before sunrise while the kids slept, to fit my inner work into my schedule. Now, decades later as the mother of adult children, I still embrace the presunrise liminal magic and I spend the first three hours of every day tending to my soul nourishment. Carving out time for self-care practices is essential to healing. Regardless of how much time you can dedicate to your practice each day, the key is in creating consistency. Make a commitment to the amount of time that feels doable, honor this agreement with yourself, and expand as you are able.

Listening to Your Inner Voice

> You are a volume in the divine book
>
> A mirror to the power that created the universe

Whatever you want, ask it of yourself

Whatever you're looking for can be found only

Inside you

—Rumi

As you explore a deeper relationship with yourself, keeping journals of your experiences is essential. The practices in this book use visualizations and guided imagery that lead you into subliminal states of consciousness. When performing the exercises, your experience may be dreamlike and surreal. Recording your feelings, thoughts, and sensations after doing a practice will allow for deeper insights and broader awareness later on.

Practice: Stream of Consciousness

Breath between beats. The empty space that holds wisdom. In the quiet pause of the page, I see what wasn't there before. In the shadow of silence, I hear the sound of nothing spoken. Yet everything revealed.

Daily journaling is an opportunity for self-expression through the power of the written word. It's a magical process of bringing your inner life to light. I learned early on about the healing power of journaling and have been using it daily since I was a teen. Without being able to put words on the page, I would be lost in a seething mess of jumbled thoughts swirling around my head. As I write each morning, the letters line up neatly like dutiful soldiers ready to fight the battles of my mind. The paper, once a strong Tree, holds my deepest secrets. The journal, a safe haven, allows me to be as I am. No right, no wrong. I don't have to worry about being inappropriate or offending anyone. This is the one place where I can say what I feel as my pen burbles a widening stream, free from guilt and shame.

This deeply insightful and rewarding practice can be done in as little as ten minutes a day.

Select a beautiful journal to be your confidante.

Choose a time of day when you're alone, without disturbances. First thing in the morning is a liminal time, when the unconscious mind is open and unaffected by outside influences.

Begin by making yourself comfortable and centering with several deep breaths.

Set a timer for ten minutes or fill two or three pages, as you engage in "stream of consciousness" writing. Allow your thoughts, feelings, and sensations to flow freely onto the page. Write about whatever feels most compelling. If you can't think of anything, write, "I can't think of anything," until words emerge. Don't worry about editing yourself. Write in ink, so it can't be erased. Tell your story without fear.

An important part of the journaling process is to reread your writings on the new and full Moon of each month, to observe any patterns and to explore new insights.

Insight Questions

How does it feel to connect with your inner voice?

What story do you want to tell?

What is something new that you learned about yourself through your writing?

Through a consistent, intentional writing practice, you discover that which is sometimes shocking, often comforting, and always your truth. I've been doing this practice for decades, and every time I reread my journals, I'm led toward new awarenesses that I couldn't otherwise have arrived at by way of intellectual terrain.

Dreams

Lucid dreaming is a captivating aspect of the human experience, offering a treasure trove of insights beyond the reach of the logical mind. Like windows into the soul, your dreams breathe life into your reality, as nocturnal journeys into the depths of the unconscious mind reveal powerful fragments of hidden wisdom.

First thing in the morning, I like to write down my dreams from the previous night, in as much detail as possible. Who was there? Where did the scene take place? What feelings did I feel? What was the atmosphere like? What would I title the dream? Images, colors, and sounds all are relevant details. When you're done writing, don't reread it until the next Moon cycle. When you go back and review what you've recorded, there are likely to be relevant symbolisms that lead to deeper understandings of your waking life. Often, I find that the questions I was struggling with work themselves out through these night visions, as the answers become clearer in time.

Sometimes dreams can be startling or even frightful. As your unconscious mind struggles to make sense of the abuse you suffered, it can be overwhelming to put words to a disturbing scenario. If writing about your dreams feels too raw or literal, you can explore the depth of imagery through art by sketching the essence of the dream. Reflect on the shapes, colors, and patterns that emerge, and trust in your process of meaning to unfold more deeply when the time is right.

Foundational Safety

> Trauma dissociates us from the parts of our body that are wounded, so we have to leave our whole body. It's a journey you take your whole life, that coming back in, relanding in your body, in yourself, on the Earth. I think one of the reasons it's been so easy, in a way, for us to violate both women and the Earth is this profound dissociation that exists in everyone.
>
> —Eve Ensler

As a small child, I can recall countless hours spent alone, in my room, my fortress of safety. Most other times, I recall feeling unsafe when with my family, at school, and in public. As a lack of a sense of safety progressed throughout my life, sometimes I would fall into the abyss of not feeling worthy of being born, and really not feeling fully incarnated in my body. A key point in my healing was when I woke up from the fog of dissociation.

As I healed my emotional wounds, I began to notice how my lack of presence manifested physically—bruises and cuts appearing from bumping into furniture or mishandling tools. I wasn't intentionally trying to harm myself; rather, I had learned this coping mechanism of disconnection from my physical form at a young age, to shield myself from the pain of abuse.

Another way that detachment from myself would show up was in getting lost in my head, obsessively ruminating on daydreams and stories. A rich fantasy life that I could navigate was empowering for a while, until the unstoppable scenes flashing on the movie screen of my mind became a way to distance myself from real life. The breakthrough came in recognizing that this habit of checking out served me as a way to escape a disturbing reality in my youth but no longer serves me as an empowered adult. The medicine was to deeply connect with my physical presence, to create an actual foundation of inner strength, in the here and now.

A Note on Chakras

As I grew stronger and more aware of my dissociative habits, I learned how to connect with my physical body by way of my energetic body. Early on, I discovered the grounding effects of being able to work with my internal source through the ancient Indian ayurvedic system, which understands the physical body as a complex network of energies. "Chakra" is a Hindu word that means spinning wheel. There are thousands of chakras in your body that make up your entire energetic system. Ancient Vedic wisdom recognizes seven specific energy centers in your vertical axis that can be attuned to, felt, and worked with to transform stuck or challenging sensations and emotions.

How do you feel about your first chakra? Not sure where it is? Sit upright in your seat and squeeze your bottom. Now release and place your attention at the base of your tailbone, where it meets the chair. That's your first chakra, also referred to as your "root." The importance of attuning to this area is to activate a sense of safety within, as you draw on the stability of this energetic resource.

Practice: Trust. Relax. Be.

This exercise came to me when I was honing my skills for grounding into my body. During a particularly enervating meditation session, I was feeling uneasy and unable to sink into my being. Suddenly the words "trust, relax, be" sang in my mind. As I breathed through this mantra, I applied it to each chakra and felt a sense of expansive grounding that became my go-to technique for initiating foundational support.

Working with the seven essential chakras, this guided meditation helps you connect with your internal power points as you ground into your body, to engage support and balance in the present moment. As you move through the energy centers, you will be guided with gentle affirmations to recite in your mind's voice.

Begin by sitting comfortably, with your feet grounding into the floor.

Place your attention on your first chakra, the root, at the base of your spine. Gently tighten your perineum and slowly release. Do this for a few breaths, tightening with each inhalation and releasing more deeply with each exhalation.

From this place of dynamic support, draw the energy downward, through your legs, down through your knees, down through your calves, down through your feet, and right down into the energy of Earth.

Continue with a few more full breaths, grounding more deeply with each inhalation and each exhalation.

Bring your attention to each chakra, as you recite the affirmations in your mind's voice:

First chakra, at the root of your spine, "*I trust that I am safe*."

Second chakra, at your lower belly, "*I trust my sexuality*."

Third chakra, at your solar plexus, "*I trust my will*."

Fourth chakra, at your heart, "*I trust love*."

Fifth chakra, at your throat, "*I trust my self-expression*."

Sixth chakra, at your third eye, "*I trust my inner knowing*."

Seventh chakra, at the crown of your head, "*I trust my highest wisdom*."

Breathe a bit more deeply into any places that feel overly active or stuck.

Bring your awareness to each chakra, as you recite the affirmations in your mind's voice:

Root, "*I relax into safety*."

Lower belly, "*I relax into sexuality*."

Solar plexus, "*I relax into will*."

Heart, "*I relax into love*."

Throat, "*I relax into self-expression*."

Third eye, "*I relax into inner knowing*."

Crown, "*I relax into wisdom*."

Breathe a bit more deeply into any places that need attention.

Breathe into each energy center, simply allowing them to just be, as they are. Take several full breaths.

Breathing more deeply into any places that feel stuck. Softening and expanding.

In your mind's voice, allow the mantra to resonate within: "*Trust. Relax. Be. Trust. Relax. Be. Trust. Relax. Be*."

Rest in this space of alignment and safety for several deep breaths. Know that when challenges arise, you can access this supportive space within, anytime you need.

Begin to gently bring your awareness back to your physical presence. Keeping your eyes soft, slowly bring your awareness back to the room you're in. On the next exhalation, open your eyes, feeling awake, refreshed, and grounded.

Insight Questions

What did you notice in your body?

When do you feel safe?

What energy centers need your attention?

Movement Leads to Change

Your physical body is the vehicle that supports you in all that you do and is the foundation of empowered, aware movement. As a sexual trauma survivor, to be able to feel into your somatic experience and attend to the energy that is alive inside you is to reclaim your body as sacred, strong, and free.

Take time each day to engage in energizing physical practices to move any stuck or excessive energy.

Dance to upbeat music. This is one of my favorite ways to move my body. Even if I don't feel "in the mood," once I turn on my favorite playlist I'm swaying to a rhythm that carries me away from feeling immobilized.

Take a brisk walk outside. Around the block, on a hiking trail, by the beach. Wherever your feet will transport you in the moment. Allow your senses to take in the elements of Nature and let the nourishment fill you.

Go for a run. If you are someone who likes to move quickly, then put on your sneakers and go. Shift stagnant energy or release pent-up feelings through the power of your dynamic activation.

To create a sense of calmness and peace in the face of anxiety, roll out your mat and slide into yoga practice. Feel your sinewy muscles, flexible and strong, as you stretch, breathe, and grow.

The ancient arts of qigong and tai chi are empowering ways to connect with and listen to your body. Through slow, deep movements, you build strength, release toxins, and enliven your life-force energy.

Imagination as a Tool for Transformation

Imagination is more important than knowledge.

—Albert Einstein

The truth is, we all constantly use our imaginations, although much of the time, many of us are imagining the worst. As trauma survivors, we can get trapped in a loop of fear and worry, limiting and sabotaging ourselves, without even knowing it. Once I became aware of my habit of anxious worry, I engaged the dynamic force of active imagination regularly. I was hooked, as I spent as little as twenty minutes each morning connecting with this limitless source of creative energy and began to approach healing sexual trauma in a whole new way—one that was easeful and, dare I say, even enjoyable.

For several months I worked with skillful coaches who taught me how to use neurolinguistic and hypnotherapeutic practices to gain mastery of my subconscious capacities through a resonant dialogue with my internal experiences. Within my physical empire was all the information I needed to discover deeper self-awareness, and the strength of mind to alchemize change. I remember feeling like I was going into the cave of my soul, well equipped, unafraid, and ready to face the dragons who'd been hiding out there since childhood. Once I learned how to locate and commune with my sensations of anger, sorrow, and fear, and to hold them without judgment, they began to transform. When I embraced my emotions as pure energy, I wanted to reach out and touch them with curiosity and reflect on them with acceptance. The challenging feelings that I so desperately tried to get rid of for so long ended up being the provocative cues that helped me understand myself better.

Empowerment over my sexual trauma began by actually seeing myself in my mind's eye as a strong, powerful being in service of my younger parts that got wounded in the past and sometimes still get triggered in the present. As my empowered adult self learned to take greater responsibility for my more fragile, vulnerable parts, I discovered the courage and strength to reparent myself, through a dimension of inner safety.

One time, I attended a workshop on the power of the unconscious mind to heal emotional trauma. Jean Shinoda Bolen, MD, is a brilliant community elder who was on the front lines of the feminist movement and has been a visionary for women's empowerment for over six decades. Her wisdom runs deep, and as I was sitting in a room with thirty other women, she led us on a metaphysical journey, with the grace and skill of a centuries-old shaman. I quickly went under, as her soft, commandeering voice brought me to a place high above the clouds, sailing along on the back of a giant Bluebird. The visualization prompt was "Who would you like to forgive?," and although I typically resent this question, since it feels like it somehow means that forgiveness is part of being victimized, this day I embraced it and went on a trip to meet with my dead father, who abused me. I'd been wrangling with this truth my entire life, and through the arduous stages of therapy, I made peace awhile ago. But what came to me this time was his sorrow and regret at having hurt me. His voice actually rang out the words, like a bell chiming my innocence. Finally, there was no question in my mind if it was my fault or what I did to deserve it. For the first time I understood his maligned actions as part of the suffering he was experiencing, part of the fault of his character, not mine. In this way, forgiveness came. Through my father's subliminal admission of wrongdoing, I forgave myself.

Navigating Triggers

> You gain strength, courage, and confidence by every experience in which you really stop to look fear in the face. You are able to say to yourself, "I have lived through this horror. I can take the next thing that comes along." You must do the thing you think you cannot do.
>
> —Eleanor Roosevelt

Anxiety, fear, depression, and anger can get triggered even years after trauma has occurred. Whether sped up or slowed down, the energy of your body holds all the information you need to attend to healing, which is why being able to recognize and attune to the emotional activations within is a foundational resource for transcending sexual abuse. Feelings are not facts, but it is vital to give your emotions a place to land, space to reflect on, and room to expand, in order to change them.

In working through emotional triggers, when an "uncomfortable" feeling arises, you can recognize that it originates from the place of your younger, more vulnerable parts and is not coming from your empowered adult self. This understanding frees up your energy, so that you're able to show up for the parts that need tender care, in the moment.

Since the essence of a trigger is to catch you off guard, it's best to use a simple self-soothing skill and return to the provoked feelings later, when there's more time and space to unpack what needs to be addressed.

Practice: Breath as Balance

Intentional breathing, always available and deeply nourishing for the nervous system, has been used for millennia to help humans reconnect with their vital life-force energy, especially when it is out of balance, or to maintain a peaceful state of equilibrium. When you experience a trigger, you can pause and engage the easeful practice of 4-4-8 breathing.

Take a deep, full breath into your belly, for four counts.

Hold the breath for four counts.

Slowly extend the exhalation, as you release for eight counts.

Repeat this pattern for a few breaths until you feel calm and centered.

Later, when the time and space allow, give yourself care. Prepare a cup of tea and sit quietly for a few minutes. Then use any of the foundational tools that you've learned how to wield. Journal, connect with Nature, move your body, or do a visualization practice. Afterward, take some time to integrate the medicine and give yourself gratitude and appreciation for taking good care.

Insight Questions

What does your breath tell you?

How can you more deeply nourish yourself?

What can you release?

Practice: Inner Dialogue

> When we encounter difficult times in our lives, often our initial strategy is to simply run away. But we find that our troubles follow us. Paradoxically, one of the best ways to heal is to turn toward that which is injured within us.
>
> —Jack Kornfield

The stages of transcending trauma are each powerful in their own way, and being able to own and process my emotions was probably the most cathartic part of my journey. Burning through the anger I felt toward my abusers took awhile. On the inside, I felt pissed off all the time. I broke a lot of plates along the way, which usually added to my sense of rage, rather than quieting it. When I look back on how much poison I was carrying, I realize that I was keeping myself hostage to the toxicity that was fed to me. To be able to communicate with my anger was a pivotal point in being able to understand, honor, accept, and ultimately release it.

Inner Dialogue is my version of a simple yet profound practice that I was first introduced to through Shakti Gawain's work, in the early eighties. In her best-selling self-help books, she was a pioneer in guiding people on how to reflect inwardly to access emotional states and communicate with hidden elements of their psyches.

Before you begin, take a few moments to reflect on a challenging emotion you recently experienced. The triggered energies of anger, fear, or sorrow are potent and usually within reach.

Begin by sitting comfortably, with your feet grounding into the floor.

Relax deeply into your body as you connect fully with your breath. With each inhalation and each exhalation, grounding down even more deeply into your being. Continuing with a steady flow of breath. Inhaling and exhaling in a gentle rhythm.

Feeling relaxed and receptive, bring to mind the challenging emotion you connected with earlier. Feel it in your body. Notice where it is, and allow all the active sensations to arise. Accepting it just as it is, without judgment.

In your mind's eye, envision yourself in your most empowered form. Clearly see yourself in detail. What does your face look like? What are you wearing? How do you carry your body? Get a clear sense of all the gleaming facets of your powerful being.

Once you have this image, go into the body of your empowered self, feeling into the strength and fortitude within. Reach down into your body, take the challenging emotion out, and hold it before you, letting it appear in whatever form it will. See the feeling, in detail, allowing it to be just as it is.

Looking out through the eyes of your empowered self, ask the emotion, "*What do you have to share with me?*," accepting the first answer as your truth. Then ask, "*What do you need in order to heal?*," accepting the first answer as your truth.

Once you have a sense of what the challenge is communicating to you, imagine your empowered self doing exactly what's asked for. Stay in this flow of care for a few breaths.

As you're ready, face the emotion again. Notice if it looks any different or has any qualities that you didn't notice before. You may thank it and ask if it has anything more to share with you. Accept whatever arises, just as it is.

When you feel complete, embrace the emotion, holding it so close that you integrate the healing essence into your being. Feel the wholeness that you've created within. Stay here for as long as you'd like. Know that this energy is always available to you, whenever you need.

Slowly begin to return to your physical presence, taking several full, deep breaths. Notice if the areas that were holding the challenging emotion are any softer or more expansive.

On the next exhalation, begin to return to the room you're in. Keeping a gentle flow of breath, slowly open your eyes, feeling awake, refreshed, and empowered.

Insight Questions

What new awareness came through this dialogue?

How can you give yourself what you need to heal?

What are you learning about yourself?

Transforming the Habit of Negative Self-Talk

Driving home one night from teaching a class on trauma, I was still in the habitual rut of replaying the minutiae of my words in my mind, picking apart everything I said, and got hung up on one small detail in particular. It doesn't matter what it was; what matters is the wake-up call I got when I caught myself in my mind's voice saying, "Why am I so stupid?" The words landed like a slap in my face, as the sting of self-doubt sent a halting chill through me. Instantly I pulled over to the side of the road, closed my eyes, and felt into my body to see where the derogatory words were coming from, so that I could digest the delusion of my perceived stupidity. I reflected on how the students thanked me for my wisdom and told me how much they enjoyed the class. I replaced the negative assumption of "not good enough" with the affirmative idea that I am in fact a skillful, empathetic teacher. This experience changed me. As I was able to replace my seething uncertainty with the confidence bestowed on me by my students, I learned to embrace a sense of self-worth that would be a betrayal to turn away from.

How worthy you feel begins in your mind. Transforming your old stories of self-effacement starts by replacing your internal dialogue with that which recognizes your strengths, successes, and positive outcomes. An essential skill that frees you from the negative psychobabble that undermines your ability to show up for yourself with loving acceptance becomes an affirmative foundation of self-confidence and esteem.

Below are some mental habits to become aware of to counteract negative thought patterns.

Notice the little slights you continually place on yourself throughout the day. When you hear the inner critic saying, "Why am I so stupid?," pause, reflect, and reframe. Instead try, "I'm still learning, so sometimes I'll make mistakes along the way." Or more simply, you can reverse the negative assumption to "I am wise!" And allow the new positive frame to guide you.

Be grateful for your body. Negative self-image is a harsh reality for many survivors, since it resonates within as self-loathing. If you find yourself obsessing over your weight, skin, breasts, chin, thighs, nose, or any other part of your physical empire, pause. Make peace with it. Create a list of all the things you appreciate about your body, or even like a little, and recognize the many ways it carries you throughout your day. Use positive affirmations such as "I am strong. I am beautiful. My body works hard and carries me far. I am graceful." Develop your own affirmations that resonate with what feels most powerful and vital about your physical form.

Refrain from absolutes. Transform "I should" or "I need to" into "I may" or "I would like to." Replace "always" and "never" with "sometimes" or "at times." This slight shift liberates you from getting stuck in a concretized view of yourself and opens up space for greater possibilities to emerge.

Make observations, not judgments. Change "I am too sensitive" into "I feel external energies easily" or reframe sentiments such as "My friend is so annoying" to "I feel annoyed when I'm with so-and-so." This awareness helps you recognize your experiences objectively, without the germ of negative discrimination.

Stop apologizing. "I'm sorry" is a negative affirmation. You are in fact, not "sorry." You are a complete being who is perfectly imperfect. If you need to take responsibility for your actions, try "I apologize for . . ." To be able to own your process of accountability through deeper awareness is the key to transforming your shortcomings.

Insight Questions

When do you notice self-judgments arise?

How does negative self-talk impact you?

What phrases can you use to shift your inner dialogue?

Inner Knowing Is Your Truth

> Every time you don't follow your inner guidance, you feel a loss of energy, loss of power, a sense of spiritual sadness.
>
> —Shakti Gawain

Cultivating your intuition is the necessary antidote for the poison of self-doubt. The essence of sexual trauma creates an atmosphere of confusion around who or what can be trusted, such that you were taught to question your own authority. As an engrained pattern of uncertainty dilutes your essential capacities of inner knowing, you entertain the self-deceptive habit of looking outside yourself for answers that can be instinctually found within.

Practice: Embrace Inner Knowing

When guiding others to learn how to more deeply trust their intuition, or when I'm checking my own inner compass, one of my favorite questions to ask is "What do I know to be true?"

When I pause to ask this question, I listen attentively to the messages being conveyed, with the assurance that what I'm subliminally experiencing is my truth.

This simple exercise focuses on two areas of your body that activate the energy of intuition. To strengthen your intuitive capacities, engage this practice each day or whenever you need to access solutions or validations.

Sit or lie down comfortably, with your eyes closed. Take several full, deep breaths.

Place your awareness on your second chakra, the space between your belly button and pubic bone—your gut. In your mind's voice, ask yourself, "What do I know to be true?" Accept the first answers that arise as your truth.

Take several full, deep breaths, integrating your knowing within.

Place your awareness on your sixth chakra, your third eye, the space between your eyebrows. In your mind's voice, ask yourself, "What do I know to be true?" Allow the first answers that arise, as your truth.

Take several full, deep breaths, integrating your knowing within.

Once you feel complete, record your insights in your journal for reflection later on.

Insight Questions

What do you know to be true?

When do you trust your intuition most?

What clouds your deeper knowing?

Turning Darkness into Light

> Everyone carries a shadow, and the less it is embodied in the individual's conscious life, the blacker and denser it is. At all counts, it forms an unconscious snag, thwarting our most well-meant intentions.
>
> —Carl Jung

Let's dive into an important facet of healing, called the "Shadow." The concept that we all have a shadow part of the psyche was a theory first developed by Swiss analytical psychologist Carl Jung in the 1930s. He did extensive work to uncover what the shadow means within the human psychic scape and how to reclaim it to create a whole sense of being, free from self-deception. Just as it sounds, the shadow is dark and mysterious, always with you, and yet hard to see, since it's hidden from your view.

Any feeling that you have for another person that holds some sort of activated charge is the essence of this invisible force. Since projection is part of what casts the shadow, the triggers usually show up in connection to someone who either annoys and infuriates you, or, alternately, someone whom you have a strong attraction to. No matter if the movement is negative or positive, it's the same energy, in that the feelings are repressed or denied, so they become triggered when aroused. The process of evaluating what feels most provoked for you is an alchemical exercise in making what is invisible and felt, seen, and transformed. Turning the crude metal of self-denial into the authentic gold of self-awareness is the energy found within the medicine of darkness.

Sometimes it still happens. I catch myself swooning over a new friend or enchanted by the spell of a fellow teacher or artist. More than appreciating their talents and attributes, I fall madly, amazed by all the wonderful assets they possess. Wait a minute! When I feel this pull down the slippery slope of overinfatuation, I remind myself to cast a net into the deep sea of my soul and reel in my own special gifts that I recognize within another.

Practice: 3-2-1 Shadow Process

Excerpted from the book *Integral Life Practice* by Ken Wilbur, this exercise is a powerful way to dialogue with your shadow, to get to know what's at the core of a provocative feeling. To be able to communicate with your shadow side requires you to work in a quiet, undisturbed space, where you can openly and honestly welcome your experience. You'll need your journal to record your insights afterward, or you can do the practice in written form, where you scribe the dialogue in the moment. Return to this practice whenever you need, and notice how your insights shift and evolve over time.

"Choose a person whom you want to work with. It's often easier to begin with a person with whom you have some difficulty (lover, friend, boss, family member). This person may irritate, disturb, annoy, or upset you. Or maybe you feel attracted to, obsessed with, infatuated with, or possessive about this person. In any case, choose someone with whom you have a strong emotional charge, whether positive or negative. Alternately, pick a dream image or a body sensation that distracts you or otherwise causes you to fixate on it. This can also be positive or negative.

You can recognize shadow in two ways. Shadow material either

Makes you negatively hypersensitive, easily triggered, reactive, irritated, angry, hurt, upset. It may keep coming up as a negative emotional tone or bad mood that pervades your life.

Makes you positively hypersensitive, easily infatuated, possessive, obsessed, overly attracted, or perhaps it becomes an ongoing idealization that structures your motivations or mood.

3: Face It

Now, imagine this person or observe the disturbance very closely, and then, using a journal to write in or an empty chair to talk to, describe the person, situation, image or sensation in vivid detail using 3rd-person pronouns such as "he," "him," "she," "her," "they," "their," "it," or "its." This is your opportunity to fully explore your experience of the disturbance, particularly what it is that bothers you about it. Take this opportunity to "let it out." The person you are describing will never see this. Don't try to use skillful language or say the right thing. Don't "sugar coat" or minimize anything—describe it as fully and in as much detail as possible.

2: Talk to It

Begin an imaginary dialogue with this object or person. Speak in 2nd-person pronouns like "you" and "yours." Here is your opportunity to enter into a relationship with the disturbance, so talk directly to this person or image as if he or she were actually there in the room with you. Tell them what bothers you about them. Ask them questions such as "Why are you doing this to me?" "What do you want from me?" "What are you trying to show me?" "What do you have to teach me?" Then, allow them to respond. Imagine what their response to these questions would be and speak the imaginary responses out loud and write them down in your journal. Allow yourself to be surprised by what emerges.

1: Be It

Now, writing or speaking in first person, using pronouns like "I," "me," and "mine," *be* this person, image or sensation. See the world, including yourself, from the perspective of the disturbance. Allow yourself to discover not only your similarities, but how you really *are* one and the same. Take on the qualities that either annoy or fascinate you. Embody the traits you described while "Facing It" in step 2. Make a statement of identification with this disturbance, "I am__________," "I am angry," "I am jealous," "I am radiant." This may feel wrong or awkward, and it should. The traits you are taking on are the traits that you have been denying in yourself. They're the traits that your psyche has been working so hard to keep in shadow.

To complete the process, gently become aware of the disowned qualities in yourself. Don't just see the world from this perspective but *feel* this previously excluded feeling until it resonates as your own. Experience the part of you that is this very trait. Avoid staying in your head and making the process abstract or conceptual: just *be* it. Become aware of the previously disowned shadow reintegrating into your body, your memory, your emotions, your subtle energies. This frees up the attention that was spent on keeping this shadow behind you or in denial."

Insight Questions

What surprised you in this process?

How does the energy of denial show up for you?

What are some of your positive traits?

The Essence of Love

How you love yourself is how you teach others to love you.

—Rupi Kaur

Every human was born into this world with an open heart, capable of profoundly loving and being loved. For most of my early life, I was confused about this truth. Since my abuse occurred at a young age, naturally my understanding of how to give and receive love was skewed. I believed that if only I could get the love I craved from a partner, parent, or friend, I would become complete and live happily ever after. Yet, experiencing betrayal from someone whom I believed loved me was a familiar heartbreak—one I found myself reliving time and again.

It wasn't until I let go of the sorrowful tune of undeserving love that I began to cultivate the essence of love from within. Through a dynamic process of learning how to give myself the essential offering of loving acceptance, I broke through the chains of self-judgment, shame, and guilt and, in this way, began to cultivate authentic love in my relationships with others.

The essence of self-love is that of complete acceptance of your total experience, especially those aspects that feel challenging. Sure, it's easy to embrace what is beautiful and well behaved, but far more difficult even to tolerate—let alone love—the parts that are messy and painful. Yet, it's the tarnished, unruly parts that need your acceptance the most in order to change. As you view your imperfections through the tender eyes of empathy and self-worth, you wholly honor, respect, and validate yourself and release the lie that you are not worthy of love.

Acts of self-love, when practiced regularly, lead to a sense of completion within, which in turn empowers you to share your fullest expression of affection with others. From this foundation of *true* love, the splintered pieces of your heart, once jagged and rough, become smooth and refined through your self-offering of unconditional love.

A Note on Bingeing

> Don't ask why the addiction; ask why the pain. To understand people's pain, you have to understand their lives. In other words, addiction is a normal response to trauma.
>
> —Gabor Mate

A lack of nurturance in one's early life, emotional as well as physical, is understood to be at the core of binge eating. As sexual trauma survivors, many of us grew up in homes where neglect was the protocol, so we didn't get the proper nutrition we needed to thrive. Even if we were fed wholesome foods, the inability to psychospiritually digest care can morph into a habit of self-abandonment through unhealthful eating habits. To be able to transform the careless patterns of bingeing is to become aware of your suffering connected to such compulsive behaviors.

What I notice about my own habits around reckless food choices is that I fall into unhealthful patterns when I feel most alone. As I pause to reflect on the energy of a craving, whether it's food, pot, shopping, TV, or scrolling, what I sense is that I want to fill myself with what I feel is missing. A void created from the absence of feeling loved since early childhood at times feels insatiable. In my mind I know that the addictive substance or behavior will not suffice, but it becomes a power play between binge and balance. When craving wins out, I know it's time to look inward for answers.

Entertain the following insight questions to begin to forge a path toward more mindful consumption:

When do I notice the energy of craving as most provoked?

What feels lacking when I overindulge myself?

What do I like about bingeing?

What healthful ways can I find to nourish myself?

As you reflect on the differences between self-indulgence and self-nurturance, you become more capable of giving yourself mindful nourishment. Discovering ways to offer yourself authentic, soul sustenance will feel rooted and right, as you experience a sense of fulfillment from that which truly feeds you.

Practice: Inner-Child Healing

Inner-child work is recognized by spiritual healers, shamans, and therapists alike as a safe, nurturing way to confront childhood trauma. Moving through the various stages of healing by connecting to your inner-child is a dynamic way to engender a sense of self-care and support. I've been fortunate over the years to have a few different guides lead me through this experience until I was able to access an empowered state of parenting my inner-child, on my own, with ease. Over time, I refined the visualization, offering it to others as one of my favorite ways to create a sense of inner nourishment or to soothe any unexpected, triggered reactions, within the secure boundaries of the imaginal realm.

When I first vowed to transcend my sexual trauma, I did this practice several times a week over the course of many months. Eventually, I got to a place where I felt what it was like to be a small child, crying alone, while being ignored by my parents. In the liminal space of my inner experience, I was able to safely process all the anger and fear that I felt in being abandoned. What I needed most was to be picked up and held. In this practice, I envisioned my empathetic adult self holding my small, vulnerable child and giving her exactly the unconditional love she needed to feel safe. This visualization was such potent medicine that now, when I get emotionally triggered, I can instantly go inward, hold the crying child, and feel at peace. That said, each time I engage the practice, I experience it differently. One day the challenge may take the form of a crying baby; another day it may be my angry teen. No matter who shows up, the essence is to trust in what arises to be held and healed.

Begin by sitting comfortably in a chair, with your feet planted into the floor beneath you. Feel yourself supported by the seat, with your root chakra grounding down through your legs, down through your feet, and connecting to the supportive energy of Earth.

From this solid foundation, take several deep, full breaths, feeling a gentle flow of your dynamic energy. With each exhalation, relax even more deeply into your being, more fully into your interior space.

From this place of connection and support, notice if there's anywhere in your body where the energy feels overly active or stuck. Simply notice what it feels like and allow it to be, just as it is.

Breathe more deeply into these areas. Releasing any tension, embracing the energy of spaciousness within. Inhaling and exhaling more deeply. Releasing any fear, embracing the energy of safety within.

When you're ready, envision yourself in your most powerful, adult form. See yourself in detail. What is your facial expression like? What are you wearing? How do you hold your body? Once you have a clear image of your adult self, go into the body of your empowered being, feeling what it feels like to embrace all of your gleaming facets.

Looking out through the eyes of your empowered adult, see yourself in a magical place, surrounded by the elements of Nature. As you enter more deeply into this enchanted realm, notice all the delightful sights, lovely sounds, delicious smells. As you look around, notice the animals that may be there with you. Allow yourself to drink in the imagery and relax into your blissful inner sanctuary.

Once you have a sense of easeful joy within your sanctuary, notice that there is a small child nearby. See them there now, however they appear before you, accepting their presence just as it is. How old are they? What do they look like? What are they doing? Notice their features in detail. Get a clear vision of what this child is like, and feel into what the child is experiencing in this moment.

Lovingly approach the child. Look directly in the child's face and tell them that you're here for them now, and that you have loving support to offer them. See their face clearly as you ask them, "What do you need from me right now?" Allow the first answers that come.

Offer the child what they ask for, as you envision your empowered adult giving them exactly what they need to feel safe, nourished, and whole. See the two of you together experiencing this loving connection. Stay with this vision for a while.

Then, go into the body of the small child. From the child's eyes, look out at the caring adult and sense their unconditional love and acceptance beaming at you. Feel what it feels like to be cherished and supported in this moment. To have your needs met in exactly the way you would like them to be. Feel how good it feels to receive what you need in order to thrive. Give yourself as much time as you'd like to experience this energy of loving support.

Once you feel complete, go into Observer position. See your empowered adult and the beloved child, together in your glorious sanctuary, united in the energy of total loving acceptance.

When you're ready, return again to the body of your empowered adult, looking out through your eyes at the small child. Take the child into your arms, holding them so close that you absorb all their love into your being. Allow yourself to rest in this space of supreme wholeness.

Take a few more deep, full breaths, fully embracing the integration. Know that this sense of supportive, unconditional love is always available within.

When you feel complete, slowly begin to bring your attention back to your physical body. Gently bring your awareness back to the room you're in. On the next exhalation, open your eyes, feeling refreshed, alert, and loved.

Insight Questions

What does your inner child need in order to grow?

What does it feel like to be an empowered adult?

How can you give yourself more nurturance?

Chapter 2
Find Allies

The people who love me don't flinch when I reveal myself to them.

For all of my childhood into young adulthood, the memories of my abuse lived in my mind as an abstract vestige, upheld by shame—a shady past that I thought should be kept secret to protect myself from further harm. If I didn't speak of it, then maybe it didn't really happen. Denial worked for a while, until I could no longer turn off the scenes that replayed over and over in my mind's eye. What I found was that when the abuse lived in darkness, it was a threat, able to attack at any unknown time. Yet, when I began to feel brave enough to coax it out into the light and acknowledge it as part of my experience, the inky stain started to fade.

To be understood by those who have survived sexual trauma is a gift of being seen, which is vital medicine for your healing. But when you share your experience with those who are not capable of empathy or, worse, those who try to gaslight you into some version of the truth that protects your abuser, it only adds to the poisonous confusion of self-loathing. Don't go to an empty well for water. When I was nineteen, I tried to tell my mother about the abuse I suffered years earlier at the hands of my brother. Her immediate response was "Can't you just forgive and forget?" This from the woman who used to tell me,

"You have to suffer to be beautiful," as she torturously raked the knots from my hair every Sunday evening throughout my childhood. I should have known better. Why did I suddenly expect her to be able to give me the support I needed now, when I had never gotten it from her before? I learned the hard way that to gain autonomy over my story, I had to go outside my family to get the validation I needed to heal.

In her article "The Essential Role of an Enlightened Witness in Society," psychologist Alice Miller posits that if someone who has suffered abuse or neglect has had either an "enlightened helper" while they were young or an "enlightened witness" when they were older, they will have a stronger foundation from which to transcend trauma. When Miller was doing research on her theory, she interviewed hundreds of people who experienced childhood abuse, and almost always found that the ones who had the easiest time repairing the damage said that there was at least one person, not necessarily a family member, whom they felt unconditionally loved and cared for. Miller states, "Through his or her presence, this person gave them a notion of trust, and of love. I call these persons helping witnesses. Many have also been lucky enough to find enlightened witnesses who helped them to recognize the injustices they suffered, to give vent to their feelings of rage, pain and indignation at what happened to them."

A big eye-opener for me during my early days of trauma recovery was about learning what to share about myself and with whom. When I was in the thick of it, I assumed that everyone was facing their childhood trauma and wanted to talk about it. Obviously, I was wrong. It took me a little while to realize that even some of my closest friends weren't prepared to talk about childhood sexual abuse. I clearly recall the shame I felt when I shared my past trauma with a new friend, as I saw the horror in her eyes. As if I were damaged, dirty, and broken, I locked away my urge to share this part of myself with others and vowed not to speak of it again. But the feelings didn't go away. They stayed inside me, festering and wanting to be heard and held by caring allies.

I experienced a healing a few months later, when I joined a local women's circle of childhood-sexual-abuse survivors. This was before the internet; I literally found a flyer on a community board near a farmers' market. It was divine timing that a support group was starting up at the local women's center right when I needed it most.

Six of us met every week for over a year, under the witness of a compassionate therapist. This was a magical combination of women who didn't have much in common, save for the fact that we all experienced childhood sexual abuse. Over the course of our time together, we created an enduring bond; a deep trust and assured knowing that we could call upon one another, for any reason, at any time. It was a soul-stirring part of my process of transcending trauma. To be held so attentively and lovingly by women whom I didn't really know but was incredibly intimate with developed my sense of trust like nothing else.

Over time, I learned that the more I was able to share about my abuse with empathetic beings, the less charge the narrative held. When I illuminated the truths of what happened to me, and became vocal about my experience, then it became a story that I could rewrite to include my power within it. This was a pivotal point in viewing my sexual trauma as a painful reality that I could reshape and grasp the victory in setting it free from eating away at me.

Tell Your Story

I became sick and tired of keeping quiet. As if I had some dirty secret. Even though I knew that most other women shared my experience, none of us spoke of it. Who were we all protecting? Our families? Our abusers? Ourselves?

It felt crucial for me to tell my story. First and foremost, to myself. Throughout my life, my journals have been my confidantes—the friends that I could share all my thoughts, feelings, fears, hopes, and dreams with and never face harsh judgments. Writing saved my life when I was younger and continues to guide me through processing the events of my adulthood. After years of keeping journals as safety nets to let my story unfold into, the timing felt right to share the account of my sexual trauma with others who knew firsthand what it was like to carry around such a burden.

My women's circle taught me so much about how to be in an empathetic connection with others who were tending to their childhood wounds, without the risk of scrutiny or exploitation. A truly alchemical process of turning pain into power, the sharing I experienced was as much about receiving as it was about giving. From the depth of becoming a compassionate vessel to hold and honor the truths of others, I found the vulnerability to allow myself to be unconditionally held in return.

Over the course of several weeks, we each took a turn to tell the story of what happened to us as small children. As I witnessed each woman's harrowing account of the abuse she suffered, my heart opened and I was able to hold them in complete compassionate embrace. No judgment, no fear, no shame. But that Tuesday evening when it was my turn to relate my trauma out loud, I felt sick to my stomach and disembodied. I hardly recall the words I spoke or even the feelings I felt as I shared the ugly details of my childhood sexual abuse. When I finished talking, what I do remember clearly is the face of each woman, eyes filled with love, transporting me to the next level of recovery. Without speaking, their looks told me that I was lovable, brave, safe, and whole—and I never felt broken again.

The Healing Circle

> A group of women can constellate a Mother morphic field when we gather together in a sacred circle. We create a "temenos," which means "sanctuary" in Greek. In a women's circle, every woman in the circle is herself and an aspect of every other woman there as well. There is no vertical hierarchy in a circle, and when a circle is a temenos, it is a safe place to tell the truth of our own feelings, perceptions, and experiences.
>
> —Jean Shinoda Bolen

The circle is an ancient symbol that denotes continuation, movement, connection, and wholeness. It embodies the essence of the infinite nature of existence. When you attune to the energy present within this source of totality, you can more easily embrace your challenges with the understanding of the greater container available for healing. In other words, the circle helps you recognize that you are not alone.

Find a circle. If you can't find one, start one. All it takes is a constellation of self-aware people who desire to come together to support one another's life journey. A small, empathetic group committed to holding space for one another's emotional needs creates a container of compassionate attention in which all healing effects are multiplied. Meet regularly and time gatherings around seasonal changes, since the cycles of the year reflect the constancy of your own inner rhythms.

Some good rules to follow when forming a supportive circle:

Create a space that inspires all to attend to personal growth and empowerment. Each time the group meets, a beautiful cloth and candle laid in the center of the circle acts as a container for each person to offer an item relevant to the season, such as a flower, rock, picture, poem, artwork, and so on.

Hold the circle as a sanctuary of loving acceptance and support for one another, allowing each other to be vulnerable.

Each time you meet, have a different person lead and share a practice or activity that's in alignment with the season.

Give each person time to share about whatever feels needed.

Mindfully listen to each other, without expectations, judgments, or unsolicited advice.

Thoughtfully voice compassionate responses when welcomed to do so.

Informal circles that gather for support through the ordinary ups and downs of life should comprise members who are able to be empathetic, self-reflective, and not actively in the throes of trauma. If you need a support group to confront active trauma, please do so under the guidance of a compassionate, competent therapist.

The Wisdom Within Vulnerability

Transcending the wounds of sexual abuse is so much about practicing fearlessness. Naturally, your instincts may be not to want to join in with others. On some unspoken level, shame spirals within the echoes of self-doubt. "*Am I enough? Am I too much? What will they think of me?*" The voices of such uncertainties can make it downright terrifying to show up and connect with others. In this way, sexual trauma breeds isolation. Isolation doesn't mean *living alone*; it means *viewing yourself as separate from others*. Survivors often fall into patterns of isolation because we see ourselves as different.

I used to be painfully introverted, such that I would avoid any participation in group settings for fear of exposure. As an armor, I would retreat inside myself—not from a sense of wanting privacy or me time, but deeply sequestered away in the abyss of absence, where I couldn't be found. In my self-imposed isolation, I was ultimately hiding from myself.

Looking back, I see how this aloneness and lack of friends made my recovery harder, but I also came to understand how this period of sheltering was necessary for me to gain inner strength before coming out. After getting to know myself better on an inner level, I became more inclined to want to look outside myself for connection. As I explored group activities, my trust in others developed and I grew into a leader who facilitates nourishing community circles. I'm still an introvert, but I can now safely let others in and confidently show up to display all my gleaming facets through the risks I continually take to be seen.

Still, I get it. For many, integration into communities isn't easy. There are so many excuses why you shouldn't reach out. Feelings of extreme vulnerability are common for most of us and complicated to resolve. Start slowly with what feels comfortable but also allow yourself to take chances with what feels appropriately uncertain. As you allow yourself to open more fully, connecting on a human level naturally begins to feel good. You recognize what it was you were missing, as a sense of belonging becomes a deeper sense of Self.

Practice: Dialogue with Vulnerability

> Owning our story can be hard but not nearly as difficult as spending our lives running from it. Embracing our vulnerabilities is risky, but not nearly as dangerous as giving up on love and belonging and joy—the experiences that make us the most vulnerable. Only when we are brave enough to explore the darkness will we discover the infinite power of our light.
>
> —Brené Brown

Allowing yourself to be vulnerable is often mistaken for weakness—something to guard against, as if sensitivity were inherently wrong or bad, and surrendering to deep emotions would only make you weaker. As I came to see my vulnerability as a tender opening for developing inner strength, I underwent a transformational process—one that revealed the power of accepting and honoring all parts of myself.

Over the years, I learned how to master the art of inner-dialogue practices by doing them often. At first I was resistant. It felt too surreal and not logical enough. I recall one healing session early on when I was having a hard time grappling with the feelings of vulnerability that were coming up. I wasn't sure how to work with the sense of extreme exposure I was having around others, so I decided to go inward to see what information was there. Once I trusted my intuition to guide me, my imagination took me to a place where I could talk with the vulnerability as I would a friend. As I welcomed in my sensitive awarenesses and listened to what they had to tell me, I became more able to activate a sense of security in my loving connections with others.

Before you begin, bring to mind a recent experience that left you feeling sensitive or vulnerable.

Begin by lying down in a quiet, peaceful place. Relax into the supportive energy of the ground beneath you.

Deeply connect with your breath, inhaling fully, extending your belly outward. Exhaling fully, releasing, drawing your belly inward. Continue with this gentle flow, taking several full, deep, cleansing breaths.

As you begin to feel your subtle body relax more deeply with each inhalation and each exhalation, notice where the energy feels stuck or energized. Breathe a bit more into these spaces.

On the next inhalation, place your attention on the area within your body that feels most sensitive, most vulnerable. Find the one spot that calls to be touched with your loving awareness. Breathing into this place, allow it to be just as it is, without trying to change it.

In your mind's eye, see yourself in your most powerful form. Notice all the details of your majestic presence.

Once you have a clear vision of yourself, go into the body of your empowered being, feeling what it feels like to be courageous and strong. Reaching into your body, bring the energy of vulnerability out in the open, so that you are facing it. Let it appear to you in whatever form it will. See the essence of vulnerability in as much detail as possible. What colors, shapes, and movements appear before you?

Once you have a strong visual sense of the energy, ask it, "What do you have to share with me?," allowing the first answers as your truth. Then ask, "What do you need in order to transform?," allowing the first answers as your truth. Stay with this wisdom for a few breaths.

When you're ready, go into Observer position and envision yourself giving the vulnerability exactly what it needs. Stay with this vision for a while, absorbing the essence of safety within.

When you feel complete, reach out to the vulnerability and receive it wholly, embracing it back into yourself as the two of you become one complete being.

Slowly bring your awareness back to your physical body. Bring your awareness back to the space you're in. Open your eyes, feeling awake, refreshed, and resilient.

Insight Questions

How does vulnerability show up for you?

What would you like to transform within yourself?

When do you feel most resilient?

Get with Your People

> It isn't blood that makes you my sister; it's how you understand my heart as though you carry it in your body.
>
> —Rupi Kaur

Finding allies isn't only about working with skilled practitioners or joining support groups. It's about finding like-minded beings who share your values, inspirations, and interests. Beyond having survived sexual trauma, you are a complete person who deserves to live your life within safe, supportive, enjoyable communities. Part of the fun of recovery is discovering who your people are.

As I began to get stronger and feel a sense of connection with other survivors, my whole world started to open up. My posture was more upright, my mind more clear, and my voice more fluid, and this showed when I went out into the world. One such local woman in my community noticed me, since I bought flowers from her farm stand every week. She was a soft-spoken, openhearted, strong, creative being, and I felt safe in her presence. After chatting together a few times, she found out that I used to be a hair stylist, and she must have thought that meant I would be good at harvesting, so she invited me to help her cut flowers on her organic farm. We met at the crack of dawn on Thursdays, each week getting closer as we worked alongside one other amid rows of Bachelor Button, Amaranth, and Black-Eyed-Susan, until one week we shared a deep bonding experience. Remember how I vowed not to speak of my sexual trauma again, for fear of scaring off potential allies? Well, one fateful day, it was my new friend who spoke to me about the childhood abuse she suffered. As we sat under Grandmother Apple Tree, both of us filled with emotion, we breathed a sigh of relief at having found another soul who shared a similar story. It was an electrifying, life-changing, me-too moment.

To begin to heal the parts of yourself that crave deeper connections with others, take some time to reflect inwardly on whom you are drawn to and why. Imagine the groups that you would like to be part of. Feel into what excites you. Who are the people that lift you up? Who are the people that drag you down? Evaluating your needs for community can also be about recognizing which people and groups no longer serve you. Once you cut the unhealthful energetic ties that bind, you open up space to welcome in those who will encourage you to have fun, grow, and thrive.

Ask yourself these questions:

When I need to talk, which friends and family members feel the safest to call?

What are some activities I'd like to do with others?

What communities or groups would I like to belong to?

Whom would I like to distance myself from?

Some ways you can begin to cultivate deeper connections:

Next time you're planning an activity you usually do alone, such as taking a walk, going shopping, or taking your lunch break, ask someone to come along with you.

Get involved in group activities that ignite your passions. This is a great way to meet like-minded beings. If you feel passionate about it, so do they.

At least once a week, pick up the phone and call a close friend or family member just to talk.

Take on a volunteer position. Check out organizations near your home; get involved in neighborhood projects.

If you live with others and find yourself in the habit of retreating to your room, make plans to have an evening where you cook a meal together. Share stories from your day as you dine.

At work or school, start a conversation with someone you've not talked with before.

Some inspirations for finding aligned communities:

Garden clubs

Libraries (yes, they still exist)

Art centers

Botanical gardens

Book clubs

Cooking classes

Yoga and meditation classes

Parks and Nature preserves

Photography classes

Anyplace that interests you

Creating Support Within

> If you fall in love with the imagination, you understand that it is a free spirit. It will go anywhere, and it can do anything.
>
> —Alice Walker

Sometimes alliances can be found through meditative journeys into your subconscious mind, where you envision and meet with imaginal inner guides.

A deeply nourishing, supportive, ancient practice calls in a "Spirit Guide" for direction and support, through active-imagination prompts.

As early on as I can remember, I used my imagination to connect with my inner companions for safety and support. To subliminally travel to places and meet with my internal allies for wisdom, protection, and guidance was foundational in sensing, *in essence*, what it felt like to be wholly supported and loved.

In the beginning, after journeying to meet with my Spirit Guides, I often wondered and have since been asked by others, "How do I know it's real?" What I came to understand is that "if you experience it, it's real." Why do we tend to disregard that which cannot be explained, if it provides us with valuable insights, awareness, and lessons? For me, some of my most inexplicable experiences have been the most profound, precious teachings, in that they were spontaneous and deep and led me to reflect more fully, way after the event ended.

Practice: Connecting with Spirit

Spirit Guides are unique to each person and may appear in any form, each time you engage the exercise. My own guides have revealed themselves to me in such manifestations as luminous Mother Moon, courageous Father Sun, wizened Goddess Hecate, and my real-life-rest-in-power Gramma Josie. Allow yourself to relax into the knowing that whoever shows up is there to offer you a supportive alliance.

Begin by sitting comfortably, with your feet grounding into the floor. Take several full, deep breaths and feel your root supported by the seat beneath you and connected to the foundation of Earth. Allow your effortless flow of breath, as you relax more deeply, with each inhalation and each exhalation.

Feel into your body, breathing a bit more completely into any areas that need your attention to gently soften and expand within. Take a few more deep, flowing breaths.

In your mind's eye, see yourself in your most confident, powerful form. Notice what you look like, in detail. What is the expression on your face? What are you wearing? How do you hold your body? What surrounds you?

Once you have a clear vision and felt sense of your empowered being, see yourself in a place that is peaceful and calm. Enter more deeply into this sacred place and notice all the sights, sounds, and sensations that surround you. Rest in this space for a while.

When you feel ready, go into the body of your empowered being, feeling what it feels like to be in this enchanted realm, ready to meet your Spirit Guide. Embrace the power and protection that is within you, here, now.

As you cross over into this magical place, feel yourself moving with curiosity toward your Spirit Guide. Looking out through the eyes of your empowered self, see them before you, in whatever form they appear. Trust the first image that emerges, just as it is.

Go right up to your guide and greet them. Looking into their eyes, let them know you're happy to be with them and that you welcome the loving acceptance that they have for you now. Feel yourself more deeply drawn into the healing presence of their unconditional love. Linger in this nourishing essence for several deep breaths, allowing yourself to fully integrate the nurturance received.

Once you have a sense of what it feels like to be met with absolute loving kindness, you may ask your guide to offer their wisdom. You can ask a specific question or simply ask if they have anything to share. "What do you have to share with me?" Allow yourself to rest in this awareness for as long as you need.

When you feel complete, thank your Spirit Guide for their wisdom and care. Reach out and embrace them, bringing all their love and support into your being. As you bid them farewell, know that you can call upon them anytime you need.

When you're ready, slowly bring your awareness back to your body and back to the room you're in. Open your eyes, feeling awake, refreshed, and nurtured.

Afterward, reflect in your journal about your experience, in as much detail as possible. You may even feel inspired to sketch your Spirit Guide to enliven and ennoble their powers of protection, wisdom, and compassion.

Insight Questions

Who showed up as your guide?

What wisdom did you receive?

How does your guide's presence manifest in your life?

How You See Yourself

Books are magic. They show up as guides when we need direction, they comfort us as friends when we need validation, and they entertain us as companions when we need camaraderie. Books have been some of my greatest teachers, and I relish each drop of wisdom culled from every page of my trusted allies.

One such book that was integral in my process of transcending trauma is *Goddesses in Everywoman* by Jean Shinoda Bolen. A Jungian analyst, Bolen has dedicated her life to the exploration of how feminine archetypes are enlivened and played out in humans. The book ennobles several ancient mythological goddesses and relates them to various modern psychological challenges.

When you reflect on the ways in which the vulnerable characters such as Persephone, Aphrodite, and Hera play out in your psyche, you can see in what ways you need to build resilience within yourself. Subsequently, when you reflect on the ways in which the powerful characters such as Athena, Artemis, and Hestia are alive within, you begin to arm yourself with the honed tools of your strengths. To be able to see your habits and traits objectively, for better and for worse, is a creative way to grow beyond your limits and shed dead skin. This is a brilliant move, away from viewing yourself as a victim and toward your identity of a thriving woman.

> A Goddess doesn't wait for someone to complete her; she knows she is already whole.
>
> —Jean Shinoda Bolen

I was at a crossroads in my life, somewhere between fertility and death. A second wave of trauma resurfaced as I faced aging and shifting roles within my family. Major life transitions often bring discomfort to old personas, and I desperately felt that I needed to explore new ways of being in the world, even though I knew that this would upset the apple cart. As I became acutely aware that my own ideas about myself were changing, I was scared to face a new reality.

Goddess work was as much about calling attention to and embracing my powerful skills (Athena the master strategist) as it was about recognizing and attending to my soft spots (Aphrodite, Goddess of love). I discovered that using an alternative lens of awareness helped me shift my perspectives, to identify whom I was growing into at the core. This was especially enlightening for my transition into an empowered being, since it gave me ways to reflect on my experiences and behaviors as a woman, through the lens of dynamic archetypes, free from the cataclysmic stereotypes connected to the cultural views of the feminine.

Wise beings have used the tradition of mythological storytelling since the beginning of time to find deeper meaning within personal experiences. Below is a list of some Goddesses from various cultures and the qualities they represent.

Consider the traits of each Goddess and notice which energies feel most relevant to you, either empowered or shunned. As you feel particularly drawn to certain virtues, let yourself roam in the imagery of each woman's prowess. You can research their characteristics further to see what alignment and lessons are available within their stories. To recognize and honor this relatedness is to know yourself better through a collective resonance of feminine wisdom.

Aphrodite (Greek): Love, Beauty

Artemis (Greek): Independence, Freedom

Athena (Greek): Courage, Strategy

Demeter (Greek): Harvest, Birth

Gaia (Greek): Earth, Life

Hecate (Greek): Magic, Shadow

Hera (Greek): Marriage, Family

Hestia (Greek): Hearth, Home

Persephone (Greek): Fertility, Growth

Bastet (Egyptian): Domesticity, Childbirth

Hathor (Egyptian): Music, Pleasure

Isis (Egyptian): Motherhood, Healing

Durga (Hindu): Protection, Strength

Kali (Hindu): Destruction, Transformation

Saraswati (Hindu): Learning, Creativity

Green Tara (Buddhist): Liberation, Action

Kuan Yin (Chinese): Compassion, Mercy

Coatlicue (Aztec): Life, Death

Xochiquetzal (Aztec): Sexuality, Flowers

Corn Mother (All Indigenous peoples, North America): Abundance, Sustenance

Spider Grandmother (Hopi, Navajo, Cherokee): Leadership, Wisdom

Oshun (Nigerian): Sensuality, Water

Brigid (Celtic): Poetry, Fire

Freyja (Norse): Fertility, Love

Practice: The Goddess Within

Reflecting more deeply on your own unique physical, emotional, and spiritual traits is a dynamic process of owning who you are in the present and aspiring to whom you wish to grow into. Many of us have special affinities for mythological women whom we relate to in character. Since childhood I was drawn to feminine archetypes that displayed both power and softness. As a young woman, a print of Botticelli's *Birth of Venus* graced my wall, and I often gazed and marveled at the energy swirling about her, as she remained peaceful and protected although naked and vulnerable. This image helped me form an energetic boundary of inner strength through the power that Venus displayed in her unfaltering presence.

This creative visualization practice helps you honor and develop the strengths within yourself that are reflected in the archetypal strengths of others.

Take a few moments to settle inwardly. As you soften your gaze, close your eyes. Connecting deeply with your breath, bring to mind a mythological female Goddess or character whom you resonate with.

In your mind's eye, see all her gleaming facets that attract you to her. Notice in detail how she holds her body, the way she moves, what her voice sounds like. What colors surround her? What patterns appear? Bask in her image for a while, feeling what it feels like to be in the divine presence of your Goddess.

Through your steady flow of breath, with each inhalation and each exhalation draw her gleaming traits into yourself. Feeling your Goddess energy enlivened within, know that you can connect with this empowered essence for support whenever you need.

Take a few more deep, nourishing breaths and slowly open your eyes, feeling refreshed, awake, and confident.

Afterward, take some time to reflect on your experience. From this new lens of awareness, you can sketch the image of your Goddess, portraying all the details of her divine presence. Trust that whoever appears before you is a guide worthy of exploring. Is your Goddess familiar to you? If so, you can research her traits to discover how her energy is alive within you, and seek ways to transform the emotional challenges that you associate with her mythology. Perhaps she's a Goddess you've never encountered before, combining different elements of various characters. Consider her individual traits to see how they each might contribute to your story. Have a light touch with this discovery process and allow space for the meanings to evolve over time.

Insight Questions

Which Goddesses or mythological characters are you most attracted to?

How do their strengths inspire you?

What traits of theirs would you like to develop within yourself?

Chapter 3
Nature Heals

I learn more about myself as I quietly exist within the realm of my non-human family. This kinship, greater and more enduring than any other I've known, holds the maps of ancient wanderings. As I travel alongside Bee, River, Cloud, and Hawk, I join with my essential lineage and cleanse my wounds.

Animism is the dominant belief held by most cultures throughout the world that each facet of Nature—plant, animal, rock, Sun, Moon, Water, Air, Fire—is alive and interconnected with every species on Earth. For thousands of years, Indigenous people have lived in ways compliant with the laws of Nature for survival's sake. Since communities maintained a deep connection with, and reverence for, the planet, I doubt that early humans experienced the epidemic of anxiety and depression we live with today. Certainly, surges of adrenaline coursed through villages in times of fear and distress, but since a foundational relationship with Nature formed the cultural underpinning, people didn't suffer the same emotional despondency and ecological demise we currently face with our modern-day divorce from Gaia.

Would you ignore your loved ones if you passed them on the street? Why then would you ignore Hummingbird hovering nearby or Lizard lazing in your path? Welcoming your nonhuman family is a daily reciprocal practice activated by simply taking notice. I'm not talking about objectifying or fetishizing the beauty found in Nature, but actually honoring the kinship that embraces all life on Earth as part of your lineage beyond human form. This can be done verbally, physically, psychically, and creatively. "Hey, Sunflower, I see the miracle in your life cycle of seed to bloom. I recognize how powerful you are, and I offer you this witnessing."

One time that I recall, back in the early '80s, my sixth-grade science teacher did an experiment with the class where he gave each student two seedlings to bring home. The assignment was to give both plants their basic needs of water and sunlight, but with one we were to give attentive adoration through praise, music, and touch, and the other we were to neglect, by speaking to it harshly or not at all. After two weeks, the result, as you can guess, was that the plant treated with kindness thrived. The one that was starved of love died.

To recognize the unique habits, traits, and needs of each greater-than-human being is to find a deep resilience that will carry you through times of uncertainty and instability. I remember how I felt as a child on warm summer nights, in awe of the illuminations of Firefly. Or at the end of a long winter when I first saw Crocus popping out of the snow. I grew up in the "Garden State" of New Jersey, and with that promising name I found myself continually seeking the world of flowers and pollinators. As soon as I could drive, I would go up to the Watchung Reservation to hike and reflect on life. Spanning nearly 2,000 acres, this former land of the Lenape people is the largest Nature preserve in the state. Marveling at the craggy rocks that jutted out from forested enclaves, I could hear the birds and touch the leaves. This is where I felt the most at ease and the most connected with the energy of those who walked this Earth for thousands of years before me. I would come here alone, on my days off from work, to gain clarity of mind and peace of soul. This is where I sorted out much of the pain that plagued me in my early adulthood.

Years later, I traveled to California with my boyfriend. Growing up on Brady Bunch reruns, I always dreamed of going to this fabled place where people dressed in bohemian style and spent most of their time outdoors. So, we went. I was in awe of the wildflowers growing rampant along the freeways, the clamor of birds in ancient trees, and the warmth of sunshine, which seemed to bestow an energetic boundary of protection over this wild land. The boyfriend didn't stick, but I vowed to someday make this magical, Tolkienesque world my home. California saved my life, there's no question about that. It was through a resonant awakening within this sacred place that I learned how to deeply connect with my community of nonhumans and feel completely held in their sustaining embrace. To truly thrive, I urge you to find your nook of Earth that feels most nourishing and enlivening. Go there often and let your heart feel the synergistic flow that pulses with the blood of every being you share the space with.

You carry Mother Earth within you. She is not outside you. Mother Earth is not just your environment. In that insight of interbeing, it is possible to have real communication with the Earth, which is the highest form of prayer.

—Thich Nhat Hanh

Practice: Haiku

The ancient art of Japanese poetry that uses three lines of seventeen syllables in a 5-7-5 pattern, Haiku highlights our symbiosis with Nature as the focal point. I write every day, and I use the stanza of Haiku when I feel deeply emotional and don't want to write in a linear way or when I can't think of what to write about. It's a satisfying process that allows me to express myself profoundly, through the lens of my nonhuman lineage.

I recently reviewed my notebook from many years ago and came across a verse I wrote the day my mother passed away.

Red roses in sand

Swept away by ocean waves

Pain is gone today

Find a quiet space where you won't be disturbed, preferably outside or indoors near a window.

Take a few moments to center yourself and soften your gaze. Use your sense perceptions to focus on what feels most inspiring in your natural environment. Once you have a clear vision of an image of Nature, close your eyes.

Focus inwardly and notice any active feelings, such as joy, sadness, excitement, boredom, love, or anger. Allow whatever arises, just as it is.

Open your eyes. Connect more deeply with your chosen image of Nature as you consider the emotions you wish to convey.

Form a five-syllable phrase that describes your feelings, sensations, and reflections. Write it down. Then do the same with a seven-syllable phrase, then again with another five-syllable phrase, forming three lines.

Stay in this creative flow for as long as you'd like, playing with the images, words, and rhythms. Create one or several Haiku related to the same subject, or explore different Nature themes. Allow the process to be inspiring, fluid, and fun.

Insight Questions

What elements of Nature do you most resonate with?

What do the nonhuman beings of Earth have to share with you?

How does your connection with Nature inspire you?

A Note on Sketching

Another fulfilling way to attune to the essence of Nature is by sketching and painting the flowers, animals, birds, bugs, and landscapes in your immediate environment. To soften your gaze and enliven your nonhuman family by translating their images through art is a dynamic way to honor them and get to know them better. As you notice the colors, patterns, shapes, and nuances of a flower or animal, you witness the specific elements that contribute to their unique traits. In this way, you develop the next level of kinship, which treats all beings as special and sacred. This practice is not about being a great artist. It's about creating a close bond with the beings of the greater-than-human world through your loving attention. A dedicated sketch book becomes a family album full of your magical experiences visiting with kindred souls.

The Energies of Sun and Moon

As I highlight the paradoxical, metaphorical essences of Sun and Moon, I reflect on the emotional polarities felt by all humans and the internal contrasts within myself. Developing deeper awareness of my dynamic differences within has allowed me to create a greater sense of balance in every way.

> Look at the immense light we call the sun. If it stops shining, the flow of our life will also stop, and so the sun is our second heart, our heart outside our body. This immense "heart" gives all life on Earth the warmth necessary for existence.
>
> –Thich Nhat Hanh

The energy of Sun governs consciousness, vitality, and power. It becomes manifest when I use my intellect to solve problems and my physical momentum to get things done. In human form, a good parental figure should bestow upon us the capacities of confidence and strength. Since my trauma includes abuse endured by my human father, it took me some time to realize that I had turned away from the shining attributes meant to lead me through life.

Through deep reflection on the metaphor of Sun as my vital life-force energy, I made conscious efforts to absorb Sun's luminosity each time I went outside. I've always loved being in the warmth of sunlight, so it was easy for me to intentionally bask in the qualities of warmth, vigor, and light. Over time, as I envisioned myself being infused with these subtle energies, I experienced a felt sense of inner support. To be able to embrace my innate essences of developed will, dynamic wisdom, and unbridled confidence has been some of the most rewarding work of reclaiming my power.

The energy of Moon governs emotions, intuition, and mystery. It becomes manifest when I receive creative inspirations or whenever I open to my feelings. It's one of the most profound energies of Nature, easily accessible, naturally attractive, and deeply nourishing, Moon has been the constant companion of all living beings ever since the dawn of time. It's been well understood for thousands of years that the luminous force of the full Moon affects all life on Earth. Flowers come into supreme bloom, baby animals grow more rapidly, tides swell, and we experience a sense of heightened awareness. The new Moon is traditionally associated with women's menstrual cycles and denotes a time of introspection and new beginnings. Earth becomes reinvented with every Moon cycle, so when I consciously connect with the waxing and waning rhythms of Moon, I flow effortlessly within the cadence of life.

On the full Moon of each month, I like to give thanks for what has come to completion during this phase, and reflect on what shall evolve in the next cycle of life. This verse came to me many years ago under the glow of the full Moon. It continually serves as a prayer that illuminates answers to questions within, through my trust in celestial guidance.

Mother Moon your seeds I sow

Tell me what I need to know

Show me where I need to grow

Bless me with your healing light

Keep me safe and far from fright

Shine your golden glow on me

As I will so it shall be

As I entertain a continual flow of my solar and lunar energetic states, I recognize the ease within this interrelationship. From this deeper self-knowledge, I can expand to include more reverence for, and greater flow within, all of Earth's quantum essences.

Living by the Laws of Nature

> Those who contemplate the beauty of the earth find reserves of strength that will endure as long as life lasts. There is something infinitely healing in the repeated refrains of nature—the assurance that dawn comes after night, and spring after winter.
>
> —Rachel Carson, *Silent Spring*

To flow effortlessly with the seasons, welcome the sacred directions, and give thanks to the elements is my natural cadence within Earth's rhythm. I cannot stress enough how an acute awareness of the continual returns of each cycle supports me in ways that feel wholly empowering and right. In recognizing my divine relationship with all beings of the natural world, I ask for reflection on how the elements, directions, and seasons each contribute to a balance of my inner states.

Since ancient times, healers have always sought harmonious partnerships with Earth's energies to inform communities about how to create sustenance and sustainability. Sadly, the idea of calling in the four directions and honoring the seasons is so far removed from modern life—these grounding practices are thought of either as sacred rituals performed only by shamans and wizards or as irrelevant and separate from the threads that weave together our human tapestry.

It's easily documented that human beings have followed the ebb of natural cycles as far back as around 4000 BCE with the flooding of the Nile in Egypt. The "Wheel of the Year" is a newer model brought into popularity in the mid-twentieth century through British pagan sects inspired by ancient Celtic practices, which regard Nature as a central part of their spiritual beliefs. To attune to the cycles of Nature is to reclaim your rightful place on the Wheel and to more deeply enjoy a fulfilling experience of life.

Several years ago, I became part of a circle of five women who formed an informal support group to witness each other's challenges and share in our joys. We did this after three of us attended a workshop that focused on the powerful energy of circles and what happens when women get together solely for the purpose of exchanging ideas, inspirations, and insights. When our circle was being initiated, we met for an introductory meeting to talk about how it would transpire. We agreed that we wanted to follow a format that was meaningful, authentic, and inclusive of Nature. We decided to follow "Wheel of the Year," to acknowledge and celebrate each of the eight annual solar events that relate to a specific cycle or season. Attunement to this continual rhythm carried our group for five years, as we revisited each season with more emotional depth and greater perceptions of how the innate cycles hold, nourish, and grow us.

With a clear understanding of the Wheel's rhythm, you naturally start integrating its patterns into your life. This wisdom is universally applicable, since these pivotal points in Earth's cycle have guided all living beings since the dawn of time. After many years of following Wheel of the Year and trusting the energy to carry me through the seasons, I recognize the greater health and harmony instilled from this awareness. Without being able to see the light at the end of the tunnel, I once dreaded the dark months of winter. Through the new lens of a cyclical flow of the year, I now embrace a firm grasp of when the seasons begin, peak, and end, only to morph into the next scene of life. I notice how my energy becomes more exultant during the longest days, and how flowers and food abundantly grow to fruition. I listen for Birdsong, Bee buzz, and Cricket chirp, and I know what the clamor, or the quiet, signals. My humanity is enlivened through alignment with the greater world around me.

Displayed below are the eight cycles of seasons in the Northern Hemisphere, divided into four solar events and four seasonal events. Since this system is relevant worldwide, to observe the seasons of the Southern Hemisphere, simply transfer the dates directly across from each holiday from the opposite side.

Samhain occurs on October 31 and is recognized as the beginning of the new year. As the third of the three harvests, it signifies completion and preparation to move into the darkest months ahead, with the shortest days and longest nights. This is known as a time for honoring our ancestors and going inward to reflect on how family patterns hold us back from growth. During this period, we can engage in spiritual practices that help shed light on our shadow elements.

Yule, or winter solstice, occurs around December 21 and is the shortest day of the year. It marks the return of the light, when the cycle moves toward the emergent longer days, and symbolizes awakening within. As the Sun begins its planetary ascent, we can embrace the energies of gratitude and joy. During this time, give thanks for what is working well, and join with others to share in the delights of the season.

Imbolc happens on February 1 and is a time of celebration as we begin to emerge out of winter. The days are a bit longer, with subtle signs of new life all around. It's a time of renewal, and we notice the stirrings of spring, with buds just beginning to form and animals rousing from sleep. We can take this opportunity to connect with the energy of possibility as we set intentions for the future and begin to sketch a plan for manifesting our goals.

Ostara, or spring equinox, occurs around March 21 and is a season of balance, when the days and nights are of equal length. It's a powerful time to sow seeds and tend to gardens, as sprouts and flowers come alive and days are noticeably longer. In this period, we can connect with the essence of life flowing through us as we are grounded in Nature's energetic embrace. This is a time to wander outside and discover the seasonal gems that are all around.

Beltane arrives on May 1 and is the period of longest days, leading up to the summer solstice. During this cycle of light-filled energy, growth abounds. We feel enlivened and inspired as our bodies and souls are deeply nourished by the abundant life force. This is a powerful time to attune to our bodies and develop physical practices that support ongoing wellness. During this season, somatic activities can energize us and bring us more fully into our being.

Litha, or summer solstice, occurs around June 21 and is the longest day of the year. It is a time of great warmth, as we celebrate Sun at its highest peak. At this pinnacle, the light begins to wane slightly each day, and we can reflect on what supports us to develop resilience and release what doesn't serve our emotional and physical health.

Lammas happens on August 1 and is the first of the three harvests. This is when we begin to see the fruits of our labor ripen, as the daylight becomes somewhat shorter. In this season of abundance, our ability to nourish ourselves becomes manifest in the foods we take in. This cycle provides opportunities to offer ourselves sustenance that reflects deep self-care.

Mabon, or fall equinox, occurs around September 21 and is the second of the three harvests. We gather that which sustains us, since day and night share equal expanse. This cycle of equilibrium, with the darker months looming ahead, is an auspicious time to gather our internal resources for managing future challenges.

Practice: Calling in the Directions and Honoring the Elements

Every time I set an intentional connection with Nature, I begin by calling in the four cardinal directions as a way to gain a clearer understanding of, and exercise an honor for, how the energies of Air, Fire, Water, and Earth support me. Early humans had no choice but to acknowledge the forces of Nature and to work within primordial rhythms for survival. Today, I encourage parents and elders to teach this basic practice to the children in their lives, in an effort to develop more-enlightened humans, inspired to oversee the care of Earth. Through honoring the elements, we recognize that all beings are interconnected within one vibrational field. By awakening this submerged wisdom, we foster planetary healing, free from the energy of destruction.

This simple exercise can be done anywhere and feels most empowering outside. For greater resonance, you can gather props to symbolize the elements. A feather for Air, a candle for Fire, a small bowl of Water, and a rock or small bowl of soil for Earth. You will also need a compass if you don't know where east is.

Stand facing east, the direction of rising Sun, and repeat, "To the east I welcome Air, energy of inspiration, learning, and curiosity."

Turn to face south and repeat, "To the south I welcome Fire, energy of transformation, change, and action."

Turn to face west and repeat, "To the west I welcome Water, energy of emotions, self-reflection, and flow."

Turn to face north and repeat, "To the north I welcome Earth, energy of protection, nourishment, and healing."

"I give thanks and honor Sun. I give thanks and honor Moon. Within their glowing light, I am balanced and whole."

Take a moment to express your personal gratitude for the elemental energies in your life.

As your inner compass guides you forward to connect more deeply with the support found in the elemental realm, it's helpful to look at how the imbalance related to each energy might show up within, and to embrace the tools that will help rebalance.

When Air is imbalanced, you may feel erratic, unfocused, and easily disturbed. Connect with your breathing to relax an agitated body and calm an overactive mind.

When Fire is imbalanced, you may sense a lack of vitality, resulting in depression and procrastination. Physical movement helps reignite your curiosity and inspiration for life.

When Water is imbalanced, you may feel that your emotions are either heightened or suppressed. Do an internal scan to see where you notice sensations in your energetic system, and engage inner dialogue to see what wants to be expressed.

When Earth is imbalanced, there may be a disconnection from your nonhuman family and the greater world around you. Activate the medicine of Nature by spending more time in gardens, parks, beaches, or your own backyard.

Insight Questions

What do you feel when you call in the directions?

How are you aligned with Nature in your daily life?

What do the elements have to teach you?

A Note on Gardens

Garden calls, like a new lover. Needing my attention to grow. I scoop up her seeds in my wanting arms and spread them beyond the hedge. The bounty extends to all. The prowess of pollination, alive and surging through shared soil. Reaching the hearts and souls of all who welcome this sacred medicine.

To tend a garden is to believe in the future, since the continual renewal of flowers signifies hope. Every time you contribute to the fertility of a patch of Earth, you nurture a source that nourishes you back. To have a successful garden, you must dance within the rhythms of Nature's sway and attune to what the plants need to thrive. Whether it's feeding or weeding, the satisfaction is the same; that of caring for a piece of life-force energy that flourishes through your devoted attention.

I often find myself wandering through my backyard while taking a break from writing, and discovering the many gems of flowers, insects, birds, and rocks while trimming some overzealous weeds or watering a thirsty shrub. This interrelationship is as important to the health of the garden as it is vital to my sense of inner peace. Even if it's simply caring for kitchen houseplants, I encourage all to give love to plant beings, and to benefit from the reciprocity of flourishing.

Practice: Rooted Flower

When asked to host a private flower therapy workshop for a group who were "gardeners more than meditators," I designed this practice as a way for them to feel the support available from flower energy, through their perceptions of active imagination. I use this exercise often when I lead now, as a first step in guiding others to experience the palpable life force of Nature.

Identifying with a symbolic flower in full bloom, this practice delightfully helps you ground into your body and feel a sense of thriving within. It can be used anytime you need to connect with your physical empire from the stability of Earth's supportive grace.

Begin by sitting comfortably, with your feet grounding into the floor beneath you.

Close your eyes and take a few moments to settle inwardly and imagine the deep soil of Earth below your feet. From this place of support, take several full, deep breaths.

On the next inhalation, bring your awareness to your root chakra, the place where your bottom meets the seat. Gently tighten your perineum, and as you exhale, slowly release, grounding more deeply into the seat, into your body, and into Earth.

With each inhalation and each exhalation, ground down more deeply into the supportive energy of your root. Feel your subtle, physical presence completely relaxing as you allow yourself to drop more fully within. Continue with your deep, slow breathing, relaxing even more deeply still.

As you feel a fuller sense of relaxation and groundedness, imagine that the seat beneath you is made of organic Earth matter, such as dirt, grass, or sand. Ground down more deeply into this place, feeling the sturdiness of Earth holding you, supporting you.

Now, in the soft gaze of your mind's eye, bring to mind a flower that you feel particularly drawn to. Envision this beautiful blossom clearly, noticing the shapes, colors, and energy it emits. Hold this divine flower in your imagination, allowing it to resonate within your being.

On the next inhalation, place your attention at the base of your spine, and as you exhale, imagine the roots of your flower drawing downward, grounding you with strength, support, and ease. Let yourself root down more fully into Earth, growing, expanding, strengthening.

From this place of grounded stability, on your next inhalation, bring the deep nourishment of Earth up through the base of your spine. A stem carrying all the nutrients you need to thrive, traveling up through your pelvis, up through your solar plexus, up through your heart. Continue the flow of energy up through your throat, up through your third eye, and straight up through the crown of your head.

Envision your flower, in full bloom, resting softly at the top of your head, as if it were a beautiful crown. Feel the energy gently pulsing with ease.

Continue your steady breathing for a few deep, full breaths. Then reverse the direction of the energy, flowing downward, carrying the light through the top of your head, down through your third eye, down through your throat, down through your heart, down through your solar plexus, down through your pelvis, down through your root, and right back into Earth.

Move upward and downward through your stem, touching each energy center slowly and steadily, in an effortless flow. Feel the steady connection between Earth and Spirit. Envision your roots deeply held in Earth, connected with your fullest flowering from above. Follow this energetic pulse for several more full, deep breaths.

As you experience the flow of energy in your body, gently bring your awareness to any places that feel uncomfortable or stuck. Breathe a little more deeply into these areas, giving them the loving support of your attentive breath. Continue with a few more deep breaths, offering the energy a bit more space to soften and expand. In your mind's voice, tell the energy that you accept it, just as it is.

Take several deep, full breaths, feeling the expansion and support you've created within. Rest into this peaceful flow of your dynamic energy. Know that you can access this powerful foundation anytime you need.

When you feel ready, slowly bring your awareness back to your physical presence, remaining peaceful and relaxed. Gently bring your awareness back to the room you're in, becoming more awake. Bring your awareness to your eyes, still keeping them soft. On the next exhalation, open your eyes, feeling alert, vibrant, and grounded.

Insight Questions

What does it feel like to be supported by Earth?

How can you cultivate a deeper sense of grounding throughout your day?

What would you like to blossom within?

Chapter 4
Embrace Wholeness

> My mission in life is not merely to survive, but to thrive; and to do so with some passion, some compassion, some humor, and some style.
>
> —Maya Angelou

To embrace a sense of wholeness does not mean to become perfect. What it does mean is to welcome your many facets as illuminations of shadows and reflections of light, which contribute to your one complete being. Authentic acceptance of all your parts is what makes you whole.

As you experience a sense of thriving, you'll want to nurture this relationship to your new way of being. Through consistency with the practices outlined in this book, you create an empowered perspective on life that will make challenges easier to manage. Still, any partnership takes effort to keep it strong and healthy. Even though you have a felt sense of transcendence within, you are still a human being, living a glorious yet sometimes painful existence on planet Earth.

When you hit an emotional roadblock, you can pause, reflect on your transformation so far, and take this as an opportunity to reset. Read over your journals, talk to someone who has witnessed your healing, and turn to Nature. Make a list of your resources, spiritual as well as material, and keep it handy for such moments of self-doubt. Attune to energy medicines that support continual growth and resilience.

Practice: Anchoring Resources

This is one of my favorite quick exercises I use if I'm feeling insecure, fearful, or unconfident. It's a basic psychospiritual practice used in hypnotherapy circles, locker rooms, backstage, and boardrooms alike. The practice draws on past positive experiences such as stabilizing in-the-moment resources in order to realize success. We all have at least a few significant lifetime achievements or many small, elated joys that we can connect with to increase our stamina in the face of adversity.

Before you begin, take a few moments to reflect on a time in your life when you felt successful and proud. Hold that experience to use as a positive resource during the practice.

Begin seated, with your feet grounding into the floor. Engage with your deep, steady flow of breathing, inhaling and exhaling completely. Continue with several more deep, flowing breaths.

Grounding more deeply into your body, feeling your energy within, notice if any places feel stuck or uncomfortable. Breathe more fully into the areas that ask for more space. Continue with several full, flowing breaths.

As you begin to feel more grounded, bring to mind your positive resource. Connect with the sense of honor that you had with this experience. See yourself, in as much detail as possible, reliving this success and feel into this wonderful sense of accomplishment. Stay here for a while, allowing the energy of this positive experience to fill you completely.

Once you feel fulfilled, begin to return to your physical presence. On your next inhalation, slowly return to the room you're in. As you open your eyes, feel alert, refreshed, and empowered.

Insight Questions

How does confidence feel in your body?

What is success?

How do you radiate positivity daily?

Meeting Resistance

If you do not change direction, you may end up where you are heading.

—Lao Tzu

Resistance to change is a natural part of any growth process. As I noticed my own deep-set patterns and engrained habits begin to transform, it felt exhilarating to be able to move about more freely in the world, and at the same time it was unsettling to my old ways of being. Through my own course of healing and from years of witnessing others, I began to correlate some common ways that emotional resistance shows up, often on the precipice of great shifts in the emotional terrain. As I became more aware of the shadowy habits that kept me stuck in the ruts, I was able to work alongside the energies to navigate a path forward.

Some ways that resistance to change show up:

Control is a form of resistance to spontaneity and disorder. Life is fluid, ever changing, and often messy. When I notice myself trying to force outcomes, rather than accepting the natural flow of things, I pause to recognize where I feel the tension and restriction in my body, and I breathe into this space. I turn my gaze inward as I envision a scene from Nature, such as a refreshing waterfall. I hear the flowing sounds, breathe in the fresh scent, and feel the supportive, erratic rhythm that nourishes me from the core. I know that as I welcome the ebbs and flows of life unrestrained, I engage a deeper sense of freedom within.

Blame is a toxic habit that keeps a focus on the wrongdoings of others. It's a form of resistance to taking responsibility for your part in the matter. When I get hurt by a friend or loved one, and I allow myself to get blindsided by resentment, my ability to see how to grow through the obstacle is clouded. That's not to say that sometimes others aren't at fault, but when I hold on to accusations, I halt the ability to learn the lesson being presented to me. Every time I notice a negative assumption about another person, I try to find how that condemnation lives inside myself. The empowered move is to be accountable for my part in the challenge, so that I can release the exhausting energy of blame and free up space for the vital medicine of acceptance.

Criticizing others, situations, or yourself is a habit that resists gratitude for what is working well. Negativity about life is an insidious pattern that spreads like a disease to everything it comes in contact with. Most of us have felt firsthand how a toxic attitude festers and becomes poison for our atmosphere, which then holds us back from seeing the sparks of positivity that surround us. When I find myself falling into a negative mindset, I take some time to review my gratitude list that I keep tucked inside my journal, where I can embrace it each day. It's dog-eared and smeared, and I created it years ago and add to it regularly, to honor a sense of optimism and appreciation for all of the productive and beneficial aspects of my life.

Practice: Create a Personal Affirmation

> When we create peace and harmony and balance in our minds, we will find it in our lives.
>
> —Louise Hay

When I was in the Bach Foundation practitioner's training program, I had to learn the distinct indications for the use of the thirty-eight Bach flower remedies. Not being fond of traditional studying, I always look for creative ways to learn. To help me remember each flower's keynotes, I started creating affirmations for the different emotional states they represent. It didn't take long for me to integrate the affirmations as part of the healing process, for myself, friends, and family, and I eventually offered them to clients to bolster the efficacy of the remedies themselves. Many years later, I developed an oracle deck with the affirmations for each flower in card form, without really knowing how the energy would land in others. When I began to see the ways in which people were interacting with the deck, trusting in the language of the flowers that were intuitively laid before them, I realized that beyond part of the process of flower therapy, the affirmations stand alone as their own therapeutic offering.

One of the most embraced affirmations I extend to trauma survivors is the one I wrote for Pine:

I am worthy and deserving of life's gifts

I release guilt and shame

I embrace my divine nature

When I lead courses on how to transform trauma, one of the homework suggestions I offer others is to craft a personal affirmation, to be embraced as the energetic remedy of hope. I ask women to do this because when we're bound to the habit of negative self-talk, unable to engage a positive mindset, we undermine our potential for growth.

In my opinion, the best awareness that affirmations provide is the ability to recognize in what ways you're stuck. Much more than promoting empowerment over your challenges, affirmative language helps you understand what literally sticks in your throat. I personally work with the art of affirmations every day, and there are some days when I just don't have faith in the positive words. This always points me in the direction of how to release my judgments, assumptions, and biases, and how to bolster my self-esteem, self-love, and self-care. If I notice that a particular sentiment feels inauthentic, then I can clearly mark my growth when I recognize the newfound ease in reciting the vow.

For many months during my recovery, I used the simple phrase "It is safe for me to be alive" to help overcome my fear of showing up in the world, being seen, and expressing myself. At first, I couldn't even recall the words without reading them in writing, which, for someone who remembers everything, was a definite red flag in my perception of self-worth. As each day progressed and I more fully absorbed the essence of safety within, the words began to flow spontaneously in my mind's voice, as I ultimately embraced the remedy of courage and made friends with the energy of fear.

Take a few moments to settle inwardly and connect with your breath. Feel into any uncomfortable energy in your body and breathe more deeply into any places that ask for more freedom.

In your journal, begin to sketch a three-line positive affirmation that reflects your innermost desires for empowerment, safety, and well-being.

Over the course of several days, shape the words until they resonate with what you wish to manifest within yourself. Embrace the affirmation as your own personal prayer. Write it on a lovely piece of paper or card and keep it somewhere you will see it often.

There is no right or wrong way to do this exercise. In fact, the words will likely shift over time, as brighter illuminations of yourself emerge. You can recraft your affirmations to reflect your growth and write new affirmations for challenges that could use a positive mindset boost.

Insight Questions

What is a negative assumption you have about yourself that you would like to shift?

What do you value about yourself?

What does the positive voice within have to say?

Self-Esteem Building 101

His name was privilege, but hers was possibility. His was the same old story, but hers was a new one about the possibility of changing a story that remains unfinished, that includes all of us, that matters so much, that we will watch but also make and tell in the weeks, months, years, decades to come.

—Rebecca Solnit

I witnessed the growth of both a daughter and a son into adulthood. My partner and I have always been keen to the oppressions and injustices woven into the nooks of even progressive communities. We couldn't escape the little bits of sexism and inequities peppered throughout our days. Most distressing and angering were the ways in which schoolteachers would praise our son for being outspoken and bold and admonish our daughter for being "bossy" and "too forward." Even though both of my kids were displaying similar traits–namely, speaking up and asking questions–we were called into the principal's office (more than once) to talk about only my daughter's behavior and how it was disruptive to the class. One such "disruption" was when my daughter went to the female middle-school principal to voice her concern that a boy was parading around a sign during recess that read "Women should be slaves to men." Instead of getting validation for calling out the blatant sexism, she was told that the boy was exercising his right to "freedom of speech."

My daughter is one of the strongest young women I know, but the messages she continues to get from the outside world sometimes lead her to unknowingly act "less than" and question her own authority. In this way, the pandemic of low self-esteem runs rampant through the collective feminine consciousness and often affects our ability to flourish and thrive.

Here are three bits of learned wisdom that I offered her, as reminders of her power to procure self-esteem and confidence, day to day:

"No" is a complete sentence. You never owe anyone an explanation for why your answer is "no." Women often overshare the reasons why we don't want to do something, out of shame, fear, and guilt. If anyone has a problem with your response, it is *their problem*.

Stop apologizing. You should say you're sorry only if you've done something that hurts someone. Accidentally brushing into someone on the elevator or, worse yet, when someone bumps into you does not constitute asking forgiveness.

Practice simplicity of gratitude toward those who are helpful. Since many of us were taught to feel undeserving of care, we might digress by minimizing our needs once help gets offered, by saying, "That's okay" or "Don't worry about it," or by "overthanking." If a need of yours is being met, whether it's your partner doing the dishes or a barista making your coffee, just authentically say, "Thank you."

When Old Wounds Feel Sore

I wish I could say that transcending sexual trauma means putting an end to the epidemic of sexual abuse. No, sexual violence and sexism will still exist and provoke you at times. Give yourself space and compassion to process the triggers as they arise. Know that you are armed with the tools of awareness, strength, and resilience.

Some simple things you can do when emotions get stirred up:

Ground into Earth. This is one of the quickest, easiest ways to find balance. Go outside; find a patch of grass, an area of sand, or a plot of soil; and let your bare feet touch the ground. Stand in "Mountain" pose, tall and rooted, and feel fed from the depth of Earth's wellspring.

Breathe. Your breath is your vital life-force energy. Usually when we're upset, we either hold our breath for fear or breathe fast and hard for anxiety. Pause, close your eyes, and take ten slow, long, deep breaths.

Move your body. When you feel either emotionally enervated or shut down, connecting with your body will bring you out of your head and give your feelings a pathway to pass through. Dance, jump, run, skip, or exercise to regain a sense of equilibrium through your somatic experience.

Nourish yourself with water. This seems intuitive, but often many of us forget to drink water when we're triggered, which leads to feeling more scattered, since your brain needs hydration to maintain focus and calm.

Talk with an ally. Pick up the phone and call someone you trust. Sometimes what you need is to talk it out with someone who will not judge, shame, or belittle you.

Remind yourself that feelings are not facts. It's crucial to recognize and process your emotions whenever they get charged, and it's also important to recognize that what arises is not the truth of the matter but is alerting you to what needs to be worked with to come back into balance.

Cry if you need to. When empowered to flow freely, grief is a beautiful, dynamic emotion that cleanses you at the soul level. To open the floodgates of suffering and give in to the torrent of despair is a significant part of any growth process.

A Note on Relationships

> Peace doesn't require two people; it requires only one. It has to be you. The problem begins and ends there.
>
> —Byron Katie

It's no secret that relationships take a lot of work to maintain. Anyone who has been in a relationship knows that alongside the many beautiful opportunities for growth come the looming possibilities of failure, shaped by the challenges each partner brings. A word of advice offered to my husband and me from a sage woman after our wedding ceremony: "Lower your expectations." After thirty years of marriage, I learned that it's even better to release them altogether. Once I let go of the notion that my partner should make me feel better, meet all of my needs for care, and never piss me off, then I became free from the daunting sense of *neediness*.

Even after decades of healing work, sometimes I still get caught in the web of painful reactivity. My stomach churns, my chest tightens, and my throat closes. It's as if the sand from the playground was flung at me from the tight little fist of my playmate. Before I know it, Thwa-Pow!! Catapulted back into that place where tantrums were the only language I had to express my needs. To redirect the skewed communication with my partner, I pause. Take a breath. Notice where I feel it in my body. And soothe the parts within that are screaming to be held. I remind myself that I don't have to take on the actions or reactions of others.

As you continue to develop deeper self-awareness and become more empowered, some of the people in your life might feel challenged by your new autonomy, especially if it questions their way of being. It's not unusual to experience shifts in your closest partnerships as you take greater possession of yourself and begin to view life through a clearer lens of positivity and possibilities. Sometimes separation is inevitable, since relationships tied to old behaviors might not fit into your transcendent life. That said, if your relationships are healthy, then oftentimes partners are willing to grow alongside you. Know that whatever relational challenges are in your path are the issues that you will most benefit from looking at more closely.

Befriend Creativity

The creative adult is the child who survived.

—Ursula K. Le Guin

We all are creative at the core, and the more you can honor and embrace this facet of being, the more you will learn about yourself through the ongoing query that comes from the act of making art. To outwardly display the authentic artistry you feel on the inside is a vital celebration of your humanity and contributes to strengthening a positive sense of Self by reflecting your innermost feelings through figurative displays. On an energetic level, art validates your experience of life, since you can tell your story of abuse within the safety of abstraction.

Physiologically, when you are absorbed in a creative flow, your attention is focused, blood pressure is lowered, and anxiety is put aside to open up space for what calls to be manifest. For trauma survivors, when untapped, this essential resource gets lost in an old story of fear and self-denial. When you see yourself as the artist of your own life, you give yourself license to view the world through varying lenses that can illuminate expansive self-awareness and create positive future outcomes.

Often we think that being creative means being proficient in a specific genre of art, so if we haven't perfected the skills of drawing, painting, sculpting, music, or dance, we feel that we can't lay claim to our innate powers of creativity. The truth is that all humans create, whether it's making intentional art or making dinner; naturally, we put our special stamp of invention on what we do. I always considered myself creative and was even told so by teachers in grade school, but it wasn't until well into adulthood that I began to claim this as part of the joy of being human, which, I see now, was hidden away in an effort to protect myself from vulnerability. It takes courage to share your gifts of self-expression, and as I've gotten to know myself better through privately engaging in artistic endeavors, I feel more confident in owning my unconventional ways of being, free from worrying about the judgments of others. This might mean wearing clothes with lovely fabrics, speaking poetically about my experiences, and garnishing my food with flowers from the garden. We all have our own innovative ways in which we perform our daily routines through our deepest sense of self-expression, and to be able to acknowledge and honor yours is part of crafting a new, liberating story.

When following your energy of creativity, start with a foundation from which to explore. Organize your inventive ideas so that you can relax into what calls to be realized, without overthinking it. Write down every inspired vision that arises. I keep a dedicated notebook of nascent concepts that I review regularly. I definitely do not follow through with every idea that intrigues me, but there are many seeds scattered along the path that germinate for a few seasons until then eventually growing into full bloom. Some of my best work started with a spark that didn't seem like much at first. The trick is to not question whether an idea is good or bad, or worth pursuing or not. Simply write it down and reread your list a couple of times a month, to cull for gems.

Igniting Inspiration

> The creative process is a process of surrender, not control.
>
> —Julia Cameron

I've often noticed that the universe has a clever way of getting my attention and offering me the wisdom I need, at exactly the right time. When I sat down to write this chapter, I was suddenly unable to attune to my creative sensibilities. The words wouldn't flow; my mind went blank; I felt bereft of inspiration and eloquence. I knew that the best thing to do was to release any expectations and simply wait for the spark to reignite itself. I put down my notebook, went outside, wandered around the garden, and let myself get lost in thoughts without even trying to put words together. The next morning when I woke, the light within was rekindled, my mind focused and clear, as the cascade of language came rushing in again.

Trusting in what wants to materialize in its own time, then allowing the energy to flow freely, is the elegant dance of inspiration. The idea is to provide a container to hold the energy of creative development, so that the muse can arrive when ready. Often, the most beautiful forms of self-expression are spontaneous and could not be activated through control or force. Letting go of the need to control, dominate, or plan the outcome was likely one of the most difficult parts of my recovery. I lived most of my life in a posttraumatic state of constant control, trying to create what I thought was safety. As I began to heal, I noticed that this hypervigilance kept me from connecting with and owning my creative energy. To claim my place as a creative being was to learn how to get out of my own way and let the muse take over. When I discovered the power in allowing the energy to flow from a higher source, without having to order it, I found opportunities to engage my artistry everywhere. I now keep handy a sketchbook for showcasing my nonhuman family, a small Haiku journal for capturing bits of poetic wisdom, watercolor paints for enlivening the Nature beings around me, oodles of found botanical materials for creating walking sticks, tiny terrariums, living displays—the list goes on and changes within the fluidity of unbridled self-expression.

Aside from approaching each day with originality and flair, reserving dedicated time for creative play is a truly nourishing facet of giving yourself what you need to thrive. You don't have to have an artist's studio to engage in creative practices. Set aside time each week to discover what feels most exciting. Some days could be spent cutting up magazines and storyboarding on the dining-room table, other days you might find yourself wandering the woods and collecting pine cones and sticks for a Nature sculpture, or perhaps organizing a weekend painting party in the garage with friends is what's called for. No matter what creative endeavor appeals to you, the effect is the same. When you continually carve out space to give yourself over to inspired visions, you grow more confident in your ongoing ability to express yourself, which creates more flow throughout all areas of your life.

Allow for Joy

These days family dinner looks more like munching on berries and tomatoes alongside Bee hum and Swallowtail swoop. I am fed directly from the nectar of life itself.

On my journey of transcending sexual trauma, I arrived at the peaceful port of thriving when I began to feel more energetically empowered, emotionally lighter, and more open to joy. As my dialogue around bodily shame shifted, I experienced a deeper sense of physical safety within, which led me to want to create nourishing, sensuous rituals throughout my week.

As you explore your needs for joyful nourishment, I encourage you to practice small doses of sensual pleasure regularly. This means engaging in anything that appeals to you through your sensory perceptions. Such as the following:

Taking a luxurious soak in the tub with flower petals and essential oils

Cutting a beautiful bouquet for your home

Indulging in a soothing massage or facial

Lighting scented candles

Making a cup of Jasmine tea, spiced chai, chocolate rooibos, or any infusions that delight your taste buds

Practice: Connect with Joy

Through the years, inner-dialogue practices have been some of my greatest experiences of self-awareness, and I still regularly embrace them as powerful healing tools. I developed this one as a way to connect with my innate sense of inner bliss. It's an exhilarating process of welcoming in and embracing the positive vibrational source of pure joy.

Begin by sitting comfortably in a chair, with your feet on the floor. Feel yourself supported by the seat, grounding down through your legs, down through your feet, and deeply connecting with the foundation of Earth.

Take several deep, full breaths. With each inhalation and each exhalation, relax even more deeply into your body.

In your mind's eye, envision yourself in your most powerful form. Notice all the details of your empowered being. What are you wearing? What is your facial expression like? How do you hold your body?

Once you have a strong sense of your empowered being, see yourself in a place that is beautiful, and notice all the details that surround you. Notice the colors, sounds, and images before you.

Once you have a strong sense of your empowered being in this magical realm, envision yourself engaging in an experience of pure joy, allowing whatever arises as the energy of bliss. Feel into this feeling and fully embrace the delight that is available to you.

As you relax into this sense of elation, go into the body of your empowered self, reach inward, and bring the joy outside you, so that you are facing it and can see it clearly in whatever form it appears. Ask a question such as "What do you have to share with me?," allowing the first answers as your truth. Then ask, "What do you need in order to grow?," allowing the first answers as your truth.

When you're ready, take the joy into your arms, holding it so close that you bring it into yourself, the two of you as one complete being. Allow yourself to rest in this space of wholeness. Always within you, know that you can access the essence of joy whenever you need.

Take a few more deep, full breaths. When you feel complete, begin to bring your awareness back to your body. Slowly bring your awareness back to the room you're in, and gently open your eyes, feeling alert, refreshed, and elated.

Insight Questions

What does joy feel like within?

How can you have more joy in your life?

What holds you back from experiencing joy?

Empowered Evolution

Owl preys. Vulture swoops. Bat devours. Within the demise, my soul joins with every being ever lived. Flowers bloom, die, reseed, and grow again. So do I.

I've been living a journey of transcending sexual trauma for my entire life. The waves have been erratic and choppy at times, but the chaos has carried me to expansive, tranquil states of peace and awe. I can honestly say that with each passing year, as I stay the course, I arrive at a locus of exponential growth.

As our physiology shifts throughout our lives, women experience the hormonal dynamics of fertility and menopause, and all the patchwork woven between these polarities. It seems that there is some sort of mechanism built into the womb that activates a torrent of power when it becomes absent from the cyclical flow of blood. Of course, the energy of flow doesn't dry up, disappear, or go away once a woman stops bleeding. In fact, the energy pulses with new life, potentially elevated by a ferocity of not giving a fuck what anyone thinks, and a determined libido to make realized that which is felt as an activated passion for creative output. This is the rise in power that women are capable of, should they choose a path of transcendence.

When my lifeblood ceased at age fifty, my world was washed anew. Any fears left over from the ominous caverns of youth became faint echoes of the past. I felt myself running excitedly toward my future, arms filled with the gifts of age. What was once shrouded in confusion and despair became enlivened with a full spectrum of dazzling colors that painted each day.

To reach menopause means to have missed thirteen consecutive menstrual cycles. When I reached this milestone, I was given a "Crone Ceremony" by the women in my circle. It was a powerful experience for each of us to witness and share how our life cycles shifted, arced, and ultimately transformed all the areas of our lives. For thousands of years, this sort of ceremony was typical among Indigenous women. A lost celebration that honors and upholds the deep wisdom of our sage, female elders can be brought back into our communities to contribute to healing the planetary wound.

Pink dashes of Sky open up to reveal the day. Broadening light that spreads over Earth like a blanket of Fire. Each morning holds the promise of sunrise. Through this expansive radiance, I awaken to the possibilities within myself.

In completing this book, I wanted to leave readers with a "foolproof" remedy against residual self-doubt and lingering despair. The one source I keep returning to, which unfailingly supports me and everyone I know, is to be one with the elements of Nature. As I type these words, my eyes gaze out the window and rest upon the mating dance of a pair of ethereal-blue Swallowtail, hovering above the food garden. My heart flips with joy as I witness the chase—the colors surreal, the intimacy laid bare before me. For a moment, I feel a flicker of embarrassment, as if I should look away, a trace of shame lingering in the air. But then, the coupling invigorates me, drawing me deeper inward and touching my soul. This is the medicine. To drink in the essence of butterfly nectar is all there is. By continually giving myself over to the awes of Nature and embracing my place within this divine love story is the greatest practice in transcending my darkest challenges, and the best way I've found to experience wholeness of being. If every other practice, philosophy, or remedy fails, walk outside, open your arms wide, look up at Sky, and welcome in Gaia's love. My guarantee: You will thrive.

Addendum
Flower Therapy for Emotional Support

There is no true healing unless there is a change in outlook, peace of mind, and inner happiness.

—Edward Bach

Flowers are one of Nature's most beautiful expressions of life-force energy, delighting us like nothing else can. Being in gardens, in parks, and on hiking trails at the very least lifts our spirits and, more deeply, repairs us on the cellular level. Simply put, most everyone feels calmer and more positive in the presence of flowers. We use floral bouquets as gifts to express love, gratitude, and devotion, and to celebrate milestones and special occasions. Flowers offer the most potent medicine of Nature's gifts, welcomed by way of their soft, endearing beauty. They draw us in like a soulmate would, since we don't question their presence in our lives and we accept their phenomenal way of being. Indeed, humans and flowers share a profoundly nourishing relationship, and this synergistic connection extends to a dynamic biofield that can be accessed for healing.

Modern-day flower therapy as we know it was developed in 1930 by British physician Dr. Edward Bach, since he clearly saw the need to offer his patients a natural healing method that was resonant, simple, and effective, with a focus on emotional states rather than physical symptoms. No doubt he knew about the twelfth-century German nun and healer Hildegard of Bingen, a mystic who was well versed in the healing properties of the plant, animal, and mineral kingdoms. Saint Hildegard wrote numerous books on such subjects, gave lectures, and taught others how to heal with herbs, flowers, and gemstones. Known to collect the morning dew from the petals of fresh blossoms, she believed that the droplets contained the potent, subtle energy of the flower. She created remedies from the condensation and gave the tinctures to people who came to her to heal from various illnesses. For thousands of years before that, Indigenous people worldwide have nurtured a profound connection with Earth energy and used their sensate wisdom to guide them more deeply in their spiritual understanding of plants as medicine.

On a physiological level, pain tells you what your body is incapable of during injury, so that you can rest and heal. If you're too quick to use interventions that mask your sensations, you run the risk of further injury. The same goes for emotional trauma. When you numb out and use habits that placate suffering, you miss out on the expansive opportunities to create change in your life.

Self-reflection is the foundation of the flower therapy system. To select the appropriate remedies, you're asked to contemplate how your suffering becomes manifest—in your body, mind, and soul. To confront challenges with such depth of awareness is, in itself, a transformational process of self-repair. What I love most about the flower therapy system is that it makes it easy and even enjoyable to attune to basic human emotional challenges. Without shame or trepidation, you can hold the energy of adversity in the highest possible regard. When you provide yourself with such a supportive container for your experiences, not only do you become better able to navigate the waves, but you connect more deeply with the wounded places that call to be held with more tenderness.

In this section of the book, you will find the indications for the use of twenty-two flower remedies to support your process of emotional well-being. These are a chosen, powerful few of my favorite North American flowers that I've used for decades, personally as well as professionally, to specifically address the various emotions connected to the looming effects of sexual trauma.

The dosage of a flower remedy is simple: two drops of a single remedy by mouth, four times a day. You can mix up to seven individual flowers in a 1-ounce dropper bottle to create a combination formula. The dosage then is four drops by mouth, four times a day. Depending on whether the emotional challenge you're experiencing is acute or chronic, the transformation will start to be noticeable anywhere from a day or two to a few weeks.

Rescue Remedy®

Cherry Plum (*Prunus cerasifera*)

Clematis (*Clematis vitalba*)

Impatiens (*Impatiens glandulifera*)

Rock Rose (*Helianthemum nummularium*)

Star of Bethlehem (*Ornithogalum umbellatum*)

I am guided by steadiness and strength.

The only combination remedy in the original Bach flower therapy system, this formula combines five flowers that each uniquely supports a sense of grounded stability. It is the go-to remedy to move any stuck or triggered energy, in the moment. You can use this ready-made elixir whenever you're faced with an emergency, accident, or unexpected emotional upset. It can be used preventively before any event that gives you a sense of extreme fear or anxiety, such as travel, family gatherings, or medical appointments. Rescue Remedy® can be used every fifteen minutes, until a sense of balance is felt. The experienced transformation is that of calm and focus, with an ability to reconnect with your core essence of inner strength and resilience.

Flowers for Grounding

Buttercup (*Ranunculus occidentalis*)

California Poppy (*Eschscholzia californica*)

Fairy Lantern (*Calochortus albus*)

Shooting Star (*Dodecatheon hendersonii*)

I am grounded in my powerful presence.

When you feel grounded within, you can walk into any given situation with confidence and poise. Conversely, when your presence feels unsettled within, you feel awkward and uncomfortable in your body, disconnected from your powerful, rooted way of being. A lack of groundedness might be experienced through feeling uncertain about the importance of your talents and skills, which creates a habit of playing it small (Buttercup). Keeping even smaller still, you may find yourself stuck perpetuating emotionally immature behaviors that continue to hinder your growth process (Fairy Lantern). Another, more vague way that a faulty foundation shows up is by not feeling fully incarnated in your body, since you're unable to connect with the support of Earth's energies (Shooting Star). Or perhaps a divorce from your spiritual alignment is felt as destabilizing, with an obsessive attraction to out-of-body and psychedelic experiences, such that you experience reality as dull and lifeless (California Poppy). To be able to connect with and activate the solid life force of your energetic root system strengthens a deeper relationship to your empowered way of being.

Buttercup: The golden glow that radiates from this tiny wildflower speaks to the activation of latent will through the illumination of confidence and self-acceptance. When you don't feel that you're good enough, you live in the shadow of your inner light. There's a feeling of lack at the core as you turn away from the value of your distinctive strengths and gifts. The transformation that Buttercup offers is felt as a fuller sense of, and honor for, the innate talents that you possess. A belief in your abilities rises as you become better able to embrace your work in the world as important in its own unique way.

California Poppy: The official flower of the Golden State of California, Poppy emits an attractive, luminous quality. Poppy addresses challenges related to a sense of spiritual materialism, with a tendency toward escapism. Those in need of this remedy obsessively seek that which fulfills and enlivens through outside sources, typically in the forms of psychedelic, astral, or overly mystical experiences. Poppy's healing energy offers a sense of spiritual sustenance that feels nourishing and satisfying within. As you become better able to fill your cup with the ethereal gold that comes from welcoming grounded experiences, the need and want for external stimuli fall away.

Fairy Lantern: At times you might get swayed by emotional immaturity, refusing to go deeper into understanding your behaviors and refuting the healing work that needs to be done. Acting from a place of your wounded inner-child, when challenges arise, you become stuck in the inability to embody adulthood. Through the habit of disintegration, you accept helplessness as your truth. The brilliance of this delicate flower lights your path of evolved maturation as you learn how to initiate responsibility and self-reliance. Fairy Lantern bestows confidence in your ability to function as a healthy, empowered adult, no longer feeling weak or dependent on others.

Shooting Star: Shooting Star reconnects us to life on Earth and our human family. Cosmic armor is the invisible protection that keeps you feeling safe in the face of perceived threats, but this disconnection from your physical body translates into a disruption of your soul experience. Shooting Star is here to lead you toward your rooted place on the planet after trauma. A conduit between the Heavens and Earth, the stellar medicine that is offered guides you to your highest spiritual incarnation.

Flowers for Focus

Filaree (*Erodium cicutarium*)

Indian Pink (*Silene californica*)

Madia (*Madia elegans*)

Rosemary (*Rosmarinus officinalis*)

I am awake and centered in this present moment.

This group of flowers assists with your ability to attune to your current experience without dwelling on the past or stressing about the future. Many trauma survivors struggle with staying in the present moment. Overthinking is a monotonous habit that clouds your ability to manage your time by taking you on a journey into the abyss of rumination and worry (Filaree). Learning how to rein in a mind that's full of thoughts, ideas, inspirations, conversations, and responsibilities can be daunting when you struggle to concentrate (Madia). An active, alert mind is one of the greatest strengths of being human, but at times you may feel dull and unable to access your mental vibrancy (Rosemary). Or perhaps a need for more order might arise as you feel engulfed by the stressors of too many responsibilities (Indian Pink). The flowers in this category guide you to find balance within your cerebral energy and allow you to rest in the peaceful space of a clear, focused mind.

Filaree: This tiny, pink wildflower is the essence of peace of mind, encouraging a broader perspective on the events of your life from a heightened ability to see the bigger picture. An offering that addresses the habits of worry, fixation on small details, and erratic thoughts that overpower your reflective wisdom. With a more balanced flow of thought patterns, you discover your strength within the arc of psychic energy as you become better able to touch your thoughts, reflect, and release them.

Indian Pink: This early-spring wildflower assists with the challenge of trying to juggle too many responsibilities at once. Indian Pink brings you to a place of inner focus, centered in your sense of supreme organization and time management. Overwhelming feelings of disarray become easeful experiences of ordered achievement.

Madia: The healing quality of this mandala-like flower is that of precision of mind. From this focal point of present-moment awareness, you become better able to bring detailed attention to your projects and visions, in order to manifest success. Madia medicine combats distraction and lack of focus. Use when you find yourself jumping from activity to activity but are not feeling fully accomplished.

Rosemary: The essence of Rosemary ignites the inner flames of vitality through a deeper sense of renewed consciousness, clarity, and alertness. A spicy flower that bridges the gap between body and mind, and physical rejuvenation is catalyzed in support of dynamic focus and mental resilience.

Flowers for Self-Expression

Cosmos (*Cosmos bipinnatus*)

Indian Paintbrush (*Castilleja miniata*)

Iris (*Iris douglasiana*)

Zinnia (*Zinnia elegans*)

I am engaged in the flow of supreme expression.

To play in the field of inspired creativity is innately part of being human and wholly honors your fullest way of being. Your powers of dynamic self-expression are alive in how you show up in the world through your unique artistic presentation. The clothes you wear, the words you speak, and the home décor you choose all display your personal, inventive flair. There may be times when you feel a sense of exhaustion, with a lack of motivation to create (Indian Paintbrush). At times you might struggle to find the eloquent language to convey your ideas and visions with depth and wisdom (Cosmos). Since creativity naturally ebbs and flows, there are bound to be periods of stagnation, when you feel disconnected from your relationship to the muse (Iris). Perhaps there's a sense of seriousness that plagues you, since you find it hard to express yourself playfully (Zinnia). Through the brilliance of these inspired flowers, you awaken your creative essence within and embrace the confidence to share your gifts of authentic artistry with others.

Cosmos: A dazzling flower that relates to the essence of creative self-expression through language, Cosmos aids with disorganized thoughts that make it hard for you to express what you wish to convey with artistry and flair. This floral ally is especially supportive for those in creative fields who rely on the written and spoken word to express depth of vision and insight. Through the brilliance of Cosmos, you develop an ability to speak with inspired lucidity, translating your highest perspectives with grace and ease. Articulate communication springs forth as thoughts are enlivened with the colorful ideas of your eloquent language.

Indian Paintbrush: A radiant red wildflower that looks just like a paintbrush popping out of the soil after a long winter; the healing essence of this striking blossom is used to counterbalance exhaustion of artistic forces. When you feel your creative impulses dried up and are unable to physically rouse yourself to the call of inspiration, Indian Paintbrush is your ally at hand. This flower leads you to reconnect with your sense of joyful motivation, and your gifts of self-expression come alive through a newfound flow of creativity.

Iris: At times, inspiration may be elusive, even though there is a desire to create. At the core, there may be an inkling that something beautiful wants to emerge, but your connection to creation evades you. When you feel a block to your flow of artistic energy, Iris leads you back toward your imagination. The radiance from Iris leads you toward your path of creativity alongside a soulful vision of life. The elegance displayed in this flower's charm becomes your power to dream and create from a deeper place of originality and talent.

Zinnia: As I gaze on the cheerful quality of Zinnia's joy-infused being, I notice the playful energy that surrounds this flower, as Bee merrily dances amid the blooms, carrying nectar and spreading bliss throughout the garden. This is the medicine offered from Zinnia, when it may be difficult to touch the jubilant energy that is inherently yours. Feeling the heaviness of life or a tendency to overwork hinders the curiosity necessary to initiate the creative process. The essence of Zinnia is felt within as lightness of spirit, with a childlike ability to experience the joys of everyday life with spontaneity, play, and wonder.

Flowers for Intimacy

Hibiscus (*Hibiscus moscheutos*)

Pink Monkeyflower (*Mimulus lewisii*)

Poison Oak (*Toxicodendron diversilobum*)

Scarlet Monkeyflower (*Mimulus cardinalis*)

Sticky Monkeyflower (*Mimulus aurantiacus*)

I am divine love at the core of my being

From the tender shoots of vulnerability emerges an empowered authenticity of your intimate experiences. It is your birthright to be able to touch your true nature of sensual pleasure, even though you may feel disconnected from this truth. Because feelings of love take on many forms, perhaps yours is to discover how to unlock a heart that's been shackled in shame and fear (Pink Monkeyflower). You're left with extreme sensitivities to physical touch, and your habit may be to refute contact, such that you've put up an impenetrable boundary to sensory experiences (Poison Oak). Or perhaps there's a noncommittal feeling driving your interactions with others, as you turn away from opportunities to go deeper in emotional connections (Sticky Monkeyflower). Confusion around the skewed perceptions of femininity might be what holds you back from recognizing your innate needs and deeper desires (Hibiscus). At the core, there may be unresolved, intense emotions that need to be expressed, to move forward toward your next stage of sensual growth (Scarlet Monkeyflower). The flowers in this category lead you to touch the deeper places within that ignite the flames of instinctive pleasure and delight.

Hibiscus: The distorted cultural ideas that favor unrealistic stereotypes of women's bodies prey on the collective human psyche, since they engender a dehumanized view of sexuality. When feelings of degradation and exploitation hold you back from your innate somatic enjoyment, whether through prior psychic, emotional, or physical abuse, Hibiscus offers glowing warmth to enliven your experience of passion. As you become more responsive to your sensual needs and desires, you experience a newfound sense of true pleasure of loving touch and interactions.

Pink Monkeyflower: This delicate-looking, drought-tolerant Desert floor flower relates to a particular fear of intimacy, rooted in a sense of guilt and unworthiness, that you may have developed in an effort to protect from further pain and rejection. The essence of Pink Monkeyflower brings a sense of safety, physical as well as emotional, that carries you forward in creating stronger bonds with others. As you begin to feel safe in taking risks, you become better able to display your inner authenticity, which leads to more-fulfilling and more-nourishing relationships.

Poison Oak: Sexual trauma causes survivors to feel disconnected from their physical being, which can create obstacles to positive vulnerability. Poison Oak addresses a type of agitation connected to physical touch. When you notice a habit of reactivity arise when intimacy is initiated, you can lean into the soothing essence of this remedy. A boundary-loving flower, Poison Oak provides a sense of balanced receptivity, which allows you to let down your guard as you welcome in fulfillment of your needs for human contact and closeness.

Scarlet Monkeyflower: This fiery-red flower is useful when you find yourself stifling intense emotions, such as anger and disappointment. As you tamp down your difficult feelings in an effort to be seen as good and agreeable, they smolder and seethe beneath the surface, straining how you communicate with others. The transformation offered from this cardinal remedy is confidence to express your breadth of emotions with clarity and candor.

Sticky Monkeyflower: At times you might experience a distorted sense of physical vulnerability, with an inability to access deeper states of intimacy. As you nurture avoidance of close relationships, unable to attune to the depth of human connection, you turn away from your true essence of love and warmth. This learned behavior may lead you to repeat patterns of sexual trauma through toxic partnerships. Sticky Monkeyflower reconnects you with your vital spark and allows you to enjoy the integration of emotional and sexual experiences, without fear.

Flowers for Ancestral Healing

Saguaro (*Carnegiea gigantea*)

Joshua Tree (*Yucca brevifolia*)

Mariposa Lily (*Calochortus leichtlinii*)

Redwood (*Sequoia sempervirens*)

I embrace the evolution of my ancestral wisdom.

This category may be the least well understood in relation to sexual trauma, since it's more of an invisible, philosophical energy rather than a felt emotion. The disease of sexual abuse indeed spans familial lineage. In recognizing this facet of ancestral inheritance, we can begin to break the chain of events. Having a clear grasp of how to work within the liminal space of those who came before us and to reach toward the future to ensure that all beings live safely within their families is the key to reparations.

Desert topography expresses a particular regenerative quality of ancient source. The medicine held within the parched landscape of sand, rock, and spiny plants is the realm of renewal. It can be felt in the dead-quiet heat of day, when everything is hushed as the surreal silence takes one back to a time before any human eye ever witnessed this soulful place.

Indigenous tribes who inhabited Desert areas for thousands of years exercised deep respect and care for the land as a means of sustenance and survival. Tribal wisdom is centered on the belief that considers everything on Earth, in varying measure, to be alive, intelligent, dangerous, and sacred. Before the genocide of the earliest known communities, elders of North American tribes shared tales and lore to guide the younger generations to live life with reverence, caution, and sustainability.

Tohono, Pima, and Seri people, the original inhabitants of what's known today as the Sonoran Desert in Arizona, were deeply attuned to the wisdom found within the Desert landscape and understood how to work with this energy to support their people. They lived within the cadence of Earth, Moon, Sun, and planets. By sharing the trials and triumphs of their experiences and recognizing the conditions that their predecessors lived through, they were able to gain perspectives that kept them thriving in such a harsh environment for thousands of years.

All the flowers in this section are native to Desert regions, save for Redwood, and are considered some of the most ancient plants on Earth. The energetic resources culled from their primordial essences have a particular quality to reach deep into the chasm of ancestral trauma and create a solid structure that bridges Indigenous sagacity with modern wisdom. To become aware that you embody all the facets of those who came before you—dirt, gems, and all—is the key to ancestral healing. As you grow through this wisdom, the suffering of your family's lineage and, ultimately, the wounding of our universal collective kin become more relieved.

Saguaro: Towering tall over dusty desert landscapes, the mighty Saguaro cactus lives 150 years or more and grows in only a few places on Earth. The short-lived, night-blooming, fragrant, white blossom of Saguaro is the Arizona state flower. The Tohono O'odham who continue to steward this land partner with parks and botanical gardens throughout the state to host festivals each summer, since harvesting the gathered fruit is still considered a-joyful excursion, offering the alchemical sustenance of nourishment and delight.

The Tohono O'odham tell stories of how Saguaro was born from a human, and they refer to individual specimens as familial beings. This perception of interconnectedness has led to the present-day protection of Saguaro, currently treated with the reverence that is rooted in early tribal wisdom.

Ancient energy of our ancestors, Saguaro strengthens our connection to the venerable traditions of the first people, as the wisdom of the elders falls upon deaf ears. The remedy grants you access to the deeper lessons of your familial soul journey, so that you become better able to translate and live by the sacred messages of your kindred spirits.

Joshua Tree: An elusive being that grows only in a couple of areas of Southern California, Joshua Tree assists us with putting a stop to inherited dysfunctional patterns. As trauma survivors, we may be prone to drug and alcohol addiction and struggle with the awareness necessary to shift such destructive, passed-down generational habits. Joshua Tree creates a container that holds compassion for our ancestors, and strength to surpass the compulsions and vices handed to you from prior generations.

Mariposa Lily: This flower assists with a feeling of disconnection from the maternal source. A sense of abandonment and neglect left over from childhood can distance you from feeling a natural bond with other women, and from your own instincts to give and receive nurturance and warmth. Since the cycles of sexual abuse plague our collective female lineage and, for many of us, span the connections we have with our physical mothers, this glorious flower elicits a sense of belonging and meaning within the matriarchal web of life. No longer stuck in the role of a motherless daughter, you become better able to reparent yourself and engender the many gleaming facets of empowered maternal energy.

Redwood: The one flower in this category that does not thrive in the Desert, stately, tall Redwood is the epitome of vitality and strength. The remedy is used when you're plagued with the inherited physical symptoms that keep you weighed down by an old story of debility and suffering. You can lean on Redwood when your body feels cumbersome, weak, or disconnected from your innate root system of resilience and stability. As you align with Redwood's stature, you become better able to attune to the majestic power of regenerative health, beyond what was handed to you from birth.

Where to Buy Flower Remedies

Patricia Kaminski and Richard Katz are the founders of the Flower Essence Society in Northern California. You can purchase individual remedies and kits through their online store. They offer a yearly membership that gives you access to their online repertory of over one hundred flower remedies, including the Bach flowers. They've been a trusted resource of flower remedy research, development, sales and education since 1979. www.fesflowers.com

Bibliography

Bach, Edward. *The Essential Writings of Dr. Edward Bach: The Twelve Healers and Other Remedies & Heal Thyself*. Vermillion, 2005.

Bass, Ellen, and Davis, Laura. *The Courage to Heal*. Harper Perennial, 1994.

Bolen, Jean Shinoda. *Goddesses in Every Woman*. Harper, 2014.

Bolen, Jean Shinoda. *The Millionth Circle*. Conari, 1999.

Brown, Brene. *The Power of Vulnerability*. Ted Talk, 2010.

Carson, Rachel. *Silent Spring*. Houghton Mifflin, 1962.

Ensler, Eve. *The Vagina Monologues*. 1996.

Gawain, Shakti. *Creative Visualization*. New World Library, 1978.

Gawain, Shakti. *Developing Intuition: Practical Guidance for Daily Life*. New World Library, 1987.

Gawain, Shakti. *Discovering Your Inner Child*. New World Library, 1989.

Gawain, Shakti. *Living in the Light: A Guide to Personal and Planetary Transformation*. New World Library, 1985.

Hay, Louise. *You Can Heal Your Life*. Hay House, 1984.

Jung, C. G. *The Undiscovered Self*. Rascher, 1957.

Kaminski, Patricia. *Flower Essence Repertory*. Flower Essence Society, 2004.

Kaminski, Patricia. *Flowers That Heal*. Newleaf, 1998.

Katie, Byron. *Loving What Is: Four Questions That Can Change Your Life*. Harmony/ Rodale, 2002.

Kaur, Rupi. *The Sun and Her Flowers*. Andrews McMeel, 2017.

Kimmerer, Robin Wall. *Braiding Sweetgrass*. Milkweed Editions, 2013.

Kolk van der, Bessel. *The Body Keeps the Score*. Penguin, 2015.

Maltz, Wendy. *The Sexual Healing Journey*. Harper Collins, 1991.

Mate, Gabor. *When the Body Says No: The Cost of Hidden Stress*. Knopf, 2011.

Miller, Alice. *The Drama of the Gifted Child: The Search for the True Self*. Basic Books, 2008.

Nhat Hahn, Thich. *Being Peace*. Parallax, 1987.

Nhat Hahn, Thich. *Interbeing*. Parallax, 1987.

Nhat Hahn, Thich. *No Mud, No Lotus: The Art of Transforming Suffering*. Parallax, 2014.

Nhat Hahn, Thich. *Peace Is Every Step: The Path of Mindfulness in Everyday Life*. Bantam, 1992.

Nhat Hahn, Thich. *Present Moment, Wonderful Moment*. Parallax, 1990.

Rosenberg, Marshall. *Non-Violent Communication*. Puddledancer, 1999.

Saalisi, Dina. *The Art of Flower Therapy*. Schiffer / REDFeather, 2024.

Saalisi, Dina. *Listening to Flowers*. Schiffer / REDFeather, 2022.

Solnit, Rebecca. *Men Explain Things to Me*. Haymarket Books, 2013.

Solnit, Rebecca. *Recollections of My Nonexistence*. Viking, 2020.

Wilber, Ken, Terry Patten, Adam Leonard, and Marco Morelli. *Integral Life Practice*. Integral Books, 2008.

Index of Practices

About the Author

Dina Saalisi is a National Board health-and-wellness coach with an advanced certificate in trauma-informed coaching. She has a hypnotherapy credential through the American Board of Hypnotherapy and is a master flower remedy practitioner through the International Bach Center. As a sexual-abuse survivor, she offers compassiontate wisdom and dynamic methods to transcend trauma. She lives in California.

http://dinasaalisi.com